OLD CREOLE DAYS

Old Creole Days

A Story of Creole Life

By
GEORGE W. CABLE

PELICAN PUBLISHING COMPANY
GRETNA 2009

Pelican Pouch edition
    First printing, January 1991
    Second printing, June 1997
    Third printing, October 2001
    Fourth printing, January 2009

Library of Congress Cataloging-in-Publication Data

Cable, George Washington, 1844-1925
    Old Creole days : a story of Creole life / by George W.
    Cable. - Pelican pbk. ed.
        p. cm.
    Reprint. Originally published: New York : Scribner,
1879.
    ISBN 978-0-88289-780-6
    1. New Orleans (La.)-History-Fiction. I. Title.
PS1244.06 1990
813'.4-dc20   89-26517
                                                    CIP

Manufactured in Canada
Published by Pelican Publishing Company, Inc.
1000 Burmaster Street, Gretna, Louisiana 70053

CONTENTS

Madame Delphine

MADAME DELPHINE.

CHAPTER I.

AN OLD HOUSE.

A FEW steps from the St. Charles Hotel, in New
Orleans, brings you to and across Canal Street, the
central avenue of the city, and to that corner where
the flower-women sit at the inner and outer edges of
the arcaded sidewalk, and make the air sweet with
their fragrant merchandise. The crowd — and if it is
near the time of the carnival it will be great — will
follow Canal Street.

But you turn, instead, into the quiet, narrow way
which a lover of Creole antiquity, in fondness for a
romantic past, is still prone to call the Rue Royale.
You will pass a few restaurants, a few auction-rooms,
a few furniture warehouses, and will hardly realize that
you have left behind you the activity and clatter of a
city of merchants before you find yourself in a region
of architectural decrepitude, where an ancient and
foreign-seeming domestic life, in second stories, over-
hangs the ruins of a former commercial prosperity, and

1

upon every thing—has settled down a long sabbath of
decay. The vehicles in the street are few in number,
and are merely passing through ; the stores are shrunk-
en into shops ; you see here and there, like a patch of
bright mould, the stall of that significant fungus, the
Chinaman. Many great doors are shut and clamped
and grown gray with cobweb ; many street windows
are nailed up ; half the balconies are begrimed and
rust-eaten, and many of the humid arches and alleys
which characterize the older Franco-Spanish piles of
stuccoed brick betray a squalor almost oriental.

Yet beauty lingers here. To say nothing of the picturesque, sometimes you get sight of comfort, sometimes of opulence, through the unlatched wicket in
some *porte-cochère* — red-painted brick pavement, foliage of dark palm or pale banana, marble or granite
masonry and blooming parterres ; or through a chink
between some pair of heavy batten window-shutters,
opened with an almost reptile wariness, your eye gets
a glimpse of lace and brocade upholstery, silver and
bronze, and much similar rich antiquity.

The faces of the inmates are in keeping ; of the
passengers in the street a sad proportion are dingy
and shabby ; but just when these are putting you off
your guard, there will pass you a woman — more
likely two or three — of patrician beauty.

Now, if you will go far enough down this old street,
you will see, as you approach its intersection with ——.
Names in that region elude one like ghosts.

However, as you begin to find the way a trifle more
open, you will not fail to notice on the right-hand side,

about midway of the square, a small, low, brick house of a story and a half, set out upon the sidewalk, as weather-beaten and mute as an aged beggar fallen asleep. Its corrugated roof of dull red tiles, sloping down toward you with an inward curve, is overgrown with weeds, and in the fall of the year is gay with the yellow plumes of the golden-rod. You can almost touch with your cane the low edge of the broad, over-hanging eaves. The batten shutters at door and window, with hinges like those of a postern, are shut with a grip that makes one's knuckles and nails feel lacerated. Save in the brick-work itself there is not a cranny. You would say the house has the lockjaw. There are two doors, and to each a single chipped and battered marble step. Continuing on down the side-walk, on a line with the house, is a garden masked from view by a high, close board-fence. You may see the tops of its fruit-trees — pomegranate, peach, banana, fig, pear, and particularly one large orange, close by the fence, that must be very old.

The residents over the narrow way, who live in a three-story house, originally of much pretension, but from whose front door hard times have removed al-most all vestiges of paint, will tell you:

"Yass, de 'ouse is in'abit; 'tis live in."

And this is likely to be all the information you get — not that they would not tell, but they cannot grasp the idea that you wish to know — until, possibly, just as you are turning to depart, your informant, in a single word and with the most evident non-appreciation of its value, drops the simple key to the whole matter:

"Dey's quadroons."

He may then be aroused to mention the better appearance of the place in former years, when the houses of this region generally stood farther apart, and that garden comprised the whole square.

Here dwelt, sixty years ago and more, one Delphine Carraze; or, as she was commonly designated by the few who knew her, Madame Delphine. That she owned her home, and that it had been given her by the then deceased companion of her days of beauty, were facts so generally admitted as to be, even as far back as that sixty years ago, no longer a subject of gossip. She was never pointed out by the denizens of the quarter as a character, nor her house as a "feature." It would have passed all Creole powers of guessing to divine what you could find worthy of inquiry concerning a retired quadroon woman; and not the least puzzled of all would have been the timid and restive Madame Delphine herself.

CHAPTER II.

MADAME DELPHINE.

DURING the first quarter of the present century, the free quadroon caste of New Orleans was in its golden age.   Earlier generations — sprung, upon the one hand, from the merry gallants of a French colonial military service which had grown gross by affiliation with Span-

ish-American frontier life, and, upon the other hand,
from comely Ethiopians culled out of the less negroi-
dal types of African live goods, and bought at the
ship's side with vestiges of quills and cowries and
copper wire still in their head-dresses, — these earlier
generations, with scars of battle or private rencontre
still on the fathers, and of servitude on the manumit-
ted mothers, afforded a mere hint of the splendor that
was to result from a survival of the fairest through
seventy-five years devoted to the elimination of the
black pigment and the cultivation of hyperian excellence and nymphean grace and beauty. Nor, if we
turn to the present, is the evidence much stronger
which is offered by the *gens de couleur* whom you may
see in the quadroon quarter this afternoon, with "Icha-
bod" legible on their murky foreheads through a vain
smearing of toilet powder, dragging their chairs down
to the narrow gateway of their close-fenced gardens,
and staring shrinkingly at you as you pass, like a nest
of yellow kittens.

But as the present century was in its second and
third decades, the *quadroones* (for we must contrive a
feminine spelling to define the strict limits of the caste
as then established) came forth in splendor. Old trav-
ellers spare no terms to tell their praises, their faultless-
ness of feature, their perfection of form, their varied
styles of beauty, — for there were even pure Caucasian
blondes among them, — their fascinating manners, their
sparkling vivacity, their chaste and pretty wit, their
grace in the dance, their modest propriety, their taste
and elegance in dress. In the gentlest and most

poetic sense they were indeed the sirens of this land, where it seemed "always afternoon " — a momentary triumph of an Arcadian over a Christian civilization, so beautiful and so seductive that it became the subject of special chapters by writers of the day more original than correct as social philosophers.

The balls that were got up for them by the male *sang-pur* were to that day what the carnival is to the present. Society balls given the same nights proved failures through the coincidence. The magnates of government, — municipal, state, federal, — those of the army, of the learned professions and of the clubs, — in short, the white male aristocracy in every thing save the ecclesiastical desk, — were there. Tickets were high-priced to insure the exclusion of the vulgar. No distinguished stranger was allowed to miss them. They were beautiful! They were clad in silken ex-tenuations from the throat to the feet, and wore, withal, a pathos in their charm that gave them a family likeness to innocence.

Madame Delphine, were you not a stranger, could have told you all about it; though hardly, I suppose, without tears.

But at the time of which we would speak (1821–22) her day of splendor was set, and her husband — let us call him so for her sake — was long dead. He was an American, and, if we take her word for it, a man of noble heart and extremely handsome; but this is knowledge which we can do without.

Even m those days the house was always shut, and Madame Delphine's chief occupation and end in life seemed to be to keep well locked up in-doors. She was an excellent person, the neighbors said, — a very worthy person; and they were, maybe, nearer correct then they knew. They rarely saw her save when she went to or returned from church; a small, rather tired-looking, dark quadroone of very good features and a gentle thoughtfulness of expression which would take long to describe: call it a widow's look.

In speaking of Madame Delphine's house, mention should have been made of a gate in the fence on the Royal-street sidewalk. It is gone now, and was out of use then, being fastened once for all by an iron staple clasping the cross-bar and driven into the post.

Which leads us to speak of another person.

CHAPTER III.

CAPITAINE LEMAITRE.

HE was one of those men that might be any age, — thirty, forty, forty-five; there was no telling from his face what was years and what was only weather. His countenance was of a grave and quiet, but also luminous, sort, which was instantly admired and ever afterward remembered, as was also the fineness of his hair and the blueness of his eyes. Those pronounced him youngest who scrutinized his face the closest. But waiving the discussion of age, he was odd, though

not with the oddness that he who had reared him
had striven to produce.

He had not been brought up by mother or father
He had lost both in infancy, and had fallen to the care
of a rugged old military grandpa of the colonial school,
whose unceasing endeavor had been to make " his
boy " as savage and ferocious a holder of unimpeachable social rank as it became a pure-blooded French
Creole to be who would trace his pedigree back to the
god Mars.

" Remember, my boy," was the adjuration received
by him as regularly as his waking cup of black coffee,
" that none of your family line ever kept the laws of
any government or creed." And if it was well that
he should bear this in mind, it was well to reiterate it
persistently, for, from the nurse's arms, the boy wore
a look, not of docility so much as of gentle, *judicial*
benevolence. The domestics of the old man's house
used to shed tears of laughter to see that look on the
face of a babe. His rude guardian addressed himself
to the modification of this facial expression ; it had not
enough of majesty in it, for instance, or of large dare-
deviltry ; but with care these could be made to come.

And, true enough, at twenty-one (in Ursin Lemaitre), the labors of his grandfather were an apparent
success. He was not rugged, nor was he loud-spoken,
as his venerable trainer would have liked to present
him to society ; but he was as serenely terrible as a
well-aimed rifle, and the old man looked upon his re-
sults with pride. He had cultivated him up to that
pitch where he scorned to practise any vice, or any

virtue, that did not include the principle of self-asser-
tion. A few touches only were wanting here and there
to achieve perfection, when suddenly the old man died.
Yet it was his proud satisfaction, before he finally lay
down, to see Ursin a favored companion and the peer,
both in courtesy and pride, of those polished gentlemen famous in history, the brothers Lafitte.

The two Lafittes were, at the time young Lemaitre
reached his majority (say 1808 or 1812), only mer-
chant-blacksmiths, so to speak, a term intended to
convey the idea of blacksmiths who never soiled their
hands, who were men of capital, stood a little higher
than the clergy, and moved in society among its auto-
crats. But they were full of possibilities, men of
action, and men, too, of thought, with already a pronounced disbelief in the custom-house. In these days
of big carnivals they would have been patented as the
dukes of Little Manchac and Barataria.

Young Ursin Lemaitre (in full the name was Lemaitre-Vignevielle) had not only the hearty friendship
of these good people, but also a natural turn for accounts ; and as his two friends were looking about them
with an enterprising eye, it easily resulted that he
presently connected himself with the blacksmithing
profession. Not exactly at the forge in the Lafittes'
famous smithy, among the African Samsons, who,
with their shining black bodies bared to the waist,
made the Rue St. Pierre ring with the stroke of their
hammers ; but as a — there was no occasion to mince
the word in those days — smuggler.

Smuggler — patriot — where was the difference?

Beyond the ken of a community to which the enforce-ment of the revenue laws had long been merely so much out of every man's pocket and dish, into the all-devouring treasury of Spain. At this date they had come under a kinder yoke, and to a treasury that at least echoed when the customs were dropped into it ; but the change was still new. What could a man be more than Capitaine Lemaitre was — the soul of honor, the pink of courtesy, with the courage of the lion, and the magnanimity of the elephant ; frank — the very exchequer of truth ! Nay, go higher still : his paper was good in Toulouse Street. To the gossips in the gaming-clubs he was the culminating proof that smug-gling was one of the sublimer virtues.

Years went by. Events transpired which have their place in history. Under a government which the com-munity by and by saw was conducted in their interest, smuggling began to lose its respectability and to grow disreputable, hazardous, and debased. In certain on-slaughts made upon them by officers of the law, some of the smugglers became murderers. The business became unprofitable for a time until the enterprising Lafittes — thinkers — bethought them of a corrective — " privateering."

Thereupon the United States Government set a price upon their heads. Later yet it became known that these outlawed pirates had been offered money and rank by Great Britain if they would join her standard, then hovering about the water-approaches to their na-tive city, and that they had spurned the bribe ; where-fore their heads were ruled out of the market, and, meeting and treating with Andrew Jackson, they were received as lovers of their country, and as compatriots fought in the battle of New Orleans at the head of their fearless men, and — here tradition takes up the tale — were never seen afterward.

Capitaine Lemaitre was not among the killed or wounded, but he was among the missing.

CHAPTER IV.

THREE FRIENDS.

THE roundest and happiest-looking priest in the city of New Orleans was a little man fondly known among his people as Père Jerome. He was a Creole and a member of one of the city's leading families. His dwelling was a little frame cottage, standing on high pillars just inside a tall, close fence, and reached by a narrow out-door stair from the green batten gate. It was well surrounded by crape myrtles, and communicated behind by a descending stair and a plank-walk with the rear entrance of the chapel over whose worshippers he daily spread his hands in benediction. The name of the street — ah! there is where light is wanting. Save the Cathedral and the Ursulines, there is very little of record concerning churches at that time, though they were springing up here and there. All there is certainty of is that Père Jerome's frame chapel was some little new-born "down-town" thing.

that may have survived the passage of years, or may
have escaped "Paxton's Directory" "so as by fire."
His parlor was dingy and carpetless ; one could smell
distinctly there the vow of poverty. His bed-chamber
was bare and clean, and the bed in it narrow and hard ;
but between the two was a dining-room that would
tempt a laugh to the lips of any who looked in. The
table was small, but stout, and all the furniture of the
room substantial, made of fine wood, and carved just
enough to give the notion of wrinkling pleasantry.
His mother's and sister's doing, Père Jerome would
explain ; they would not permit this apartment—or
department—to suffer. Therein, as well as in the
parlor, there was odor, but of a more epicurean sort,
that explained interestingly the Père Jerome's rotund-
ity and rosy smile.

In this room, and about this miniature round table,
used sometimes to sit with Père Jerome two friends to
whom he was deeply attached—one, Evariste Varrillat, a playmate from early childhood, now his brother-
in-law ; the other, Jean Thompson, a companion from
youngest manhood, and both, like the little priest himself, the regretful rememberers of a fourth comrade
who was a comrade no more. Like Père Jerome, they
had come, through years, to the thick of life's conflicts,
—the priest's brother-in-law a physician, the other an
attorney, and brother-in-law to the lonely wanderer,—
yet they loved to huddle around this small board, and
be boys again in heart while men in mind. Neither
one nor another was leader. In earlier days they had
always yielded to him who no longer met with them a

certain chieftainship, and they still thought of him and talked of him, and, in their conjectures, groped after him, as one of whom they continued to expect greater things than of themselves.

They sat one day drawn thus close together, sipping and theorizing, speculating upon the nature of things in an easy, bold, sophomoric way, the conversation for the most part being in French, the native tongue of the doctor and priest, and spoken with facility by Jean Thompson the lawyer, who was half Américain ; but running sometimes into English and sometimes into mild laughter. Mention had been made of the absentee.

Père Jerome advanced an idea something like this :

"It is impossible for any finite mind to fix the degree of criminality of any human act or of any human life. The Infinite One alone can know how much of our sin is chargeable to us, and how much to our brothers or our fathers. We all participate in one another's sins. There is a community of responsibility attaching to every misdeed. No human since Adam —nay, nor Adam himself—ever sinned entirely to himself. And so I never am called upon to contemplate a crime or a criminal but I feel my conscience pointing at me as one of the accessories."

"In a word," said Evariste Varrillat, the physician, "you think we are partly to blame for the omission of many of your Paternosters, eh ? "

Father Jerome smiled.

"No ; a man cannot plead so in his own defence; our first father tried that, but the plea was not al-

lowed. But, now, there is our absent friend. I tell
you truly this whole community ought to be recognized
as partners in his moral errors. Among another people, reared under wiser care and with better companions, how different might he not have been! How
can *we* speak of him as a law-breaker who might have
saved him from that name?" Here the speaker turned
to Jean Thompson, and changed his speech to English. "A lady sez to me to-day: 'Père Jerome, 'ow
dat is a dreadfool dat 'e gone at de coas' of Cuba to
be one corsair! Ain't it?' 'Ah, madame,' I sez,
' 'tis a terrible! I 'ope de good God will fo'give me
an' you fo' dat!'"

Jean Thompson answered quickly:

"You should not have let her say that."

"*Mais*, fo' w'y?"

"Why, because, if you are partly responsible, you
ought so much the more to do what you can to shield
his reputation. You should have said," — the attorney changed to French, — "'He is no pirate; he has
merely taken out letters of marque and reprisal under the flag of the republic of Carthagena!'"

"*Ah, bah!*" exclaimed Doctor Varrillat, and both
he and his brother-in-law, the priest, laughed.

"Why not?" demanded Thompson.

"Oh!" said the physician, with a shrug, "say id
thad way iv you wand."

Then, suddenly becoming serious, he was about to
add something else, when Père Jerome spoke.

"I will tell you what I could have said. I could
have said: 'Madame, yes; 'tis a terrible fo' him. He

stum'le in de dark; but dat good God will mek it a *mo' terrible* fo' dat man oohever he is, w'at put 'at light out!' "

"But how do you know he is a pirate?" demanded Thompson, aggressively.

"How do we know?" said the little priest, returning to French. "Ah! there is no other explanation of the ninety-and-nine stories that come to us, from every port where ships arrive from the north coast of Cuba, of a commander of pirates there who is a marvel of courtesy and gentility " — [1]

"And whose name is Lafitte," said the obstinate attorney.

"And who, nevertheless, is not Lafitte," insisted Père Jerome.

"Daz troo, Jean," said Doctor Varrillat. "We hall know daz troo."

Père Jerome leaned forward over the board and spoke, with an air of secrecy, in French.

"You have heard of the ship which came into port here last Monday. You have heard that she was boarded by pirates, and that the captain of the ship himself drove them off."

"An incredible story," said Thompson.

"But not so incredible as the truth. I have it from a passenger. There was on the ship a young girl who was very beautiful. She came on deck, where the corsair stood, about to issue his orders, and, more beautiful than ever in the desperation of the moment confronted him with a small missal spread open, and

---

[1] See gazettes of the period.

her finger on the Apostles' Creed, commanded him to
read. He read it, uncovering his head as he read, then
stood gazing on her face, which did not quail; and
then with a low bow, said: 'Give me this book and I
will do your bidding.' She gave him the book and
bade him leave the ship, and he left it unmolested."

Père Jerome looked from the physician to the attorney and back again, once or twice, with his dimpled
smile.

"But he speaks English, they say," said Jean
Thompson.

"He has, no doubt, learned it since he left us,"
said the priest.

"But this ship-master, too, says his men called him
Lafitte."

"Lafitte? No. Do you not see? It is your brother-
in-law, Jean Thompson! It is your wife's brother!
Not Lafitte, but" (softly) "Lemaitre! Lemaitre!
Capitaine Ursin Lemaitre!"

The two guests looked at each other with a growing
drollery on either face, and presently broke into a laugh.

"Ah!" said the doctor, as the three rose up, "you
juz kip dad cog-an'-bull fo' yo' negs summon."

Père Jerome's eyes lighted up —

"I goin' to do it!"

"I tell you," said Evariste, turning upon him with
sudden gravity, "iv dad is troo, I tell you w'ad is
sure-sure! Ursin Lemaitre din kyare nut'n fo' doze
creed; *he fall in love!*"

Then, with a smile, turning to Jean Thompson, and
back again to Père Jerome:

"But anny'ow you tell it in dad summon dad 'e
kyare fo' dad creed."

Père Jerome sat up late that night, writing a letter.
The remarkable effects upon a certain mind, effects
which we shall presently find him attributing solely to
the influences of surrounding nature, may find for some
a more sufficient explanation in the fact that this letter
was but one of a series, and that in the rover of doubted
identity and incredible eccentricity Père Jerome had a
regular correspondent.

CHAPTER V.

THE CAP FITS.

ABOUT two months after the conversation just given,
and therefore somewhere about the Christmas holidays
of the year 1821, Père Jerome delighted the congrega-
tion of his little chapel with the announcement that he
had appointed to preach a sermon in French on the
following sabbath — not there, but in the cathedral.

He was much beloved. Notwithstanding that among
the clergy there were two or three who shook their heads
and raised their eyebrows, and said he would be at
least as orthodox if he did not make quite so much of
the Bible and quite so little of the dogmas, yet "the
common people heard him gladly." When told, one
day, of the unfavorable whispers, he smiled a little
and answered his informant, — whom he knew to be

one of the whisperers himself,—laying a hand kindly
upon his shoulder :

"Father Murphy,"—or whatever the name was,—
"your words comfort me."

"How is that?"

"Because — ' *Væ quum benedixerint mihi homi-
nes!* ' " [1]

The appointed morning, when it came, was one of
those exquisite days in which there is such a universal
harmony, that worship rises from the heart like a
spring.

"Truly," said Père Jerome to the companion who
was to assist him in the mass, "this is a sabbath day
which we do not have to make holy, but only to *keep*
so."

Maybe it was one of the secrets of Père Jerome's
success as a preacher, that he took more thought as to
how he should feel, than as to what he should say.

The cathedral of those days was called a very plain
old pile, boasting neither beauty nor riches ; but to
Père Jerome it was very lovely ; and before its homely
altar, not homely to him, in the performance of those
solemn offices, symbols of heaven's mightiest truths,
in the hearing of the organ's harmonies, and the yet
more elegant interunion of human voices in the choir,
in overlooking the worshipping throng which knelt
under the soft, chromatic lights, and in breathing the
sacrificial odors of the chancel, he found a deep and
solemn joy ; and yet I guess the finest thought of his
soul the while was one that came thrice and again :

[1] "Woe unto me when all men speak well of me!"

"Be not deceived, Père Jerome, because saintliness of feeling is easy here; you are the same priest who overslept this morning, and over-ate yesterday, and will, in some way, easily go wrong to-morrow and the day after."

He took it with him when — the *Veni Creator* sung — he went into the pulpit. Of the sermon he preached, tradition has preserved for us only a few brief sayings, but they are strong and sweet.

"My friends," he said, — this was near the beginning, — "the angry words of God's book are very merciful — they are meant to drive us home; but the tender words, my friends, they are sometimes terrible! Notice these, the tenderest words of the tenderest prayer that ever came from the lips of a blessed martyr — the dying words of the holy Saint Stephen, 'Lord, lay not this sin to their charge.' Is there nothing dreadful in that? Read it thus: 'Lord, lay not this sin to *their* charge.' Not to the charge of them who stoned him? To whose charge then? Go ask the holy Saint Paul. Three years afterward, praying in the temple at Jerusalem, he answered that question: 'I stood by and consented.' He answered for himself only; but the Day must come when all that wicked council that sent Saint Stephen away to be stoned, and all that city of Jerusalem, must hold up the hand and say: 'We, also, Lord — we stood by.' Ah! friends, under the simpler meaning of that dying saint's prayer for the pardon of his murderers is hidden the terrible truth that we all have a share in one another's sins."

Thus Père Jerome touched his key-note. All that

time has spared us beside may be given in a few sen
tences.

"Ah!" he cried once, "if it were merely my own
sins that I had to answer for, I might hold up my head
before the rest of mankind; but no, no, my friends —
we cannot look each other in the face, for each has
helped the other to sin. Oh, where is there any room,
in this world of common disgrace, for pride? Even
if we had no common hope, a common despair ought
to bind us together and forever silence the voice of
scorn!"

And again, this:

"Even in the promise to Noë, not again to destroy
the race with a flood, there is a whisper of solemn
warning. The moral account of the antediluvians was
closed off and the balance brought down in the year
of the deluge; but the account of those who come after
runs on and on, and the blessed bow of promise itself
warns us that God will not stop it till the Judgment
Day! O God, I thank thee that that day must come at
last, when thou wilt destroy the world, and stop the
interest on my account!"

It was about at this point that Père Jerome noticed,
more particularly than he had done before, sitting
among the worshippers near him, a small, sad-faced
woman, of pleasing features, but dark and faded, who
gave him profound attention. With her was another in
better dress, seemingly a girl still in her teens, though
her face and neck were scrupulously concealed by a
heavy veil, and her hands, which were small, by gloves.

"Quadroones," thought he, with a stir of deep pity.

Once, as he uttered some stirring word, he saw the mother and daughter (if such they were), while they still bent their gaze upon him, clasp each other's hand fervently in the daughter's lap. It was at these words:

"My friends, there are thousands of people in this city of New Orleans to whom society gives the ten commandments of God with all the *nots* rubbed out! Ah! good gentlemen! if God sends the poor weakling to purgatory for leaving the right path, where ought some of you to go who strew it with thorns and briers!"

The movement of the pair was only seen because he watched for it. He glanced that way again as he said:

"O God, be very gentle with those children who would be nearer heaven this day had they never had a father and mother, but had got their religious training from such a sky and earth as we have in Louisiana this holy morning! Ah! my friends, nature is a big-print catechism!"

The mother and daughter leaned a little farther forward, and exchanged the same spasmodic hand-pressure as before. The mother's eyes were full of tears.

"I once knew a man," continued the little priest, glancing to a side aisle where he had noticed Evariste and Jean sitting against each other, "who was carefully taught, from infancy to manhood, this single only principle of life: defiance. Not justice, not righteousness, not even gain; but defiance: defiance to God, defiance to man, defiance to nature, defiance to reason; defiance and defiance and defiance."

"He is going to tell it!" murmured Evariste to Jean.

"This man," continued Père Jerome, "became a smuggler and at last a pirate in the Gulf of Mexico. Lord, lay not that sin to his charge alone! But a strange thing followed. Being in command of men of a sort that to control required to be kept at the austerest distance, he now found himself separated from the human world and thrown into the solemn companicnship with the sea, with the air, with the storm, the calm the heavens by day, the heavens by night. My friends, that was the first time in his life that he ever found himself in really good company.

"Now, this man had a great aptness for accounts. He had kept them — had rendered them. There was beauty, to him, in a correct, balanced, and closed account. An account unsatisfied was a deformity. The result is plain. That man, looking out night after night upon the grand and holy spectacle of the starry deep above and the watery deep below, was sure to find himself, sooner or later, mastered by the convic tion that the great Author of this majestic creation keeps account of it; and one night there came to him, like a spirit walking on the sea, the awful, silent question: 'My account with God — how does it stand?' Ah! friends, that is a question which the book of nature does not answer.

"Did I say the book of nature is a catechism? Yes. But, after it answers the first question with 'God,' nothing but questions follow; and so, one day, this man gave a ship full of merchandise for one little book which answered those questions. God help him to understand it! and God help you, monsieur, and you, madame, sitting here in your *smuggled clothes*, to beat upon the breast with me and cry, 'I, too, Lord—-I, too, stood by and consented.'"

Père Jerome had no⊁ intended these for his closing words; but just there, straight away before his sight and almost at the farthest door, a man rose slowly from his seat and regarded him steadily with a kind, bronzed, sedate face, and the sermon, as if by a sign of command, was ended. While the *Credo* was being chanted he was still there; but when, a moment after its close, the eye of Père Jerome returned in that direction, his place was empty.

As the little priest, his labor done and his vestments changed, was turning into the Rue Royale and leaving the cathedral out of sight, he just had time to understand that two women were purposely allowing him to overtake them, when the one nearer him spoke in the Creole *patois*, saying, with some timid haste:

"Good-morning, Père—Père Jerome; Père Jerome, we thank the good God for that sermon."

"Then, so do I," said the little man. They were the same two that he had noticed when he was preaching. The younger one bowed silently; she was a beautiful figure, but the slight effort of Père Jerome's kind eyes to see through the veil was vain. He would presently have passed on, but the one who had spoken before said:

"I thought you lived in the Rue des Ursulines."

"Yes; but I am going this way to see a sick person."

The woman looked up at him with an expression of mingled confidence and timidity.

" It must be a blessed thing to be so useful as to be needed by the good God," she said.

Père Jerome smiled :

"God does not need me to look after his sick ; but he allows me to do it, just as you let your little boy in frocks carry in chips." He might have added that he 'oved to do it, quite as much.

It was plain the woman had somewhat to ask, and was trying to get courage to ask it.

" You have a little boy?" asked the priest.

" No, I have only my daughter ; " she indicated the girl at her side. Then she began to say something else, stopped, and with much nervousness asked :

"Père Jerome, what was the name of that man?"

"His name?" said the priest. " You wish to know his name?"

" Yes, Monsieur " (or *Miché*, as she spoke it) ; " it was such a beautiful story." The speaker's companion looked another way.

" His name," said Father Jerome, — " some say one name and some another. Some think it was Jean Lafitte, the famous ; you have heard of him? And do you go to my church, Madame —— ?"

" No, Miché ; not in the past ; but from this time, yes. My name " — she choked a little, and yet it evidently gave her pleasure to offer this mark of confidence — " is Madame Delphine — Delphine Carraze."

CHAPTER VI.

A CRY OF DISTRESS.

PÈRE JEROME's smile and exclamation, as some days later he entered his parlor in response to the announcement of a visitor, were indicative of hearty greeting rather than surprise.

" Madame Delphine ! "

Yet surprise could hardly have been altogether absent, for though another Sunday had not yet come around, the slim, smallish figure sitting in a corner, looking very much alone, and clad in dark attire, which seemed to have been washed a trifle too often, was Delphine Carraze on her second visit. And this, he was confident, was over and above an attendance in the confessional, where he was sure he had recognized her voice.

She rose bashfully and gave her hand, then looked to the floor, and began a faltering speech, with a swallowing motion in the throat, smiled weakly and commenced again, speaking, as before, in a gentle, low note, frequently lifting up and casting down her eyes while shadows of anxiety and smiles of apology chased each other rapidly across her face. She was trying to ask his advice.

" Sit down," said he ; and when they had taken seats she resumed, with downcast eyes :

" You know, — probably I should have said this in the confessional, but " —

"No matter, Madame Delphine; I understand; you did not want an oracle, perhaps; you want a friend."

She lifted her eyes, shining with tears, and dropped them again.

"I"— she ceased. "I have done a"— she dropped her head and shook it despondingly — "a cruel thing." The tears rolled from her eyes as she turned away her face.

Père Jerome remained silent, and presently she turned again, with the evident intention of speaking at length.

"It began nineteen years ago — by"— her eyes, which she had lifted, fell lower than ever, her brow and neck were suffused with blushes, and she murmured — "I fell in love."

She said no more, and by and by Père Jerome replied:

"Well, Madame Delphine, to love is the right of every soul. I believe in love. If your love was pure and lawful I am sure your angel guardian smiled upon you; and if it was not, I cannot say you have nothing to answer for, and yet I think God may have said "She is a quadroone; all the rights of her womanhood trampled in the mire, sin made easy to her — almost compulsory,— charge it to account of whom it may concern."

"No, no!" said Madame Delphine, looking up quickly, "some of it might fall upon"— Her eyes fell, and she commenced biting her lips and nervously pinching little folds in her skirt. "He was good — as good as the law would let him be — better, indeed, for he left me property, which really the strict law does not allow. He loved our little daughter very much. He wrote to his mother and sisters, owning all his error and asking them to take the child and bring her up. I sent her to them when he died, which was soon after, and did not see my child for sixteen years. But we wrote to each other all the time, and she loved me. And then — at last" — Madame Delphine ceased speaking, but went on diligently with her agitated fingers, turning down foolish hems lengthwise of her lap.

"At last your mother-heart conquered," said Père Jerome.

She nodded.

"The sisters married, the mother died; I saw that even where she was she did not escape the reproach of her birth and blood, and when she asked me to let her come" — The speaker's brimming eyes rose an instant. "I know it was wicked, but — I said, come."

The tears dripped through her hands upon her dress.

"Was it she who was with you last Sunday?"

"Yes."

"And now you do not know what to do with her?"

"*Ah! c'est ça oui!* — that is it."

"Does she look like you, Madame Delphine?"

"Oh, thank God, no! you would never believe she was my daughter, she is white and beautiful!"

"You thank God for that which is your main diffi culty, Madame Delphine."

"Alas! yes."

Père Jerome laid his palms tightly across his knees with his arms bowed out, and fixed his eyes upon the ground, pondering.

"I suppose she is a sweet, good daughter?" said he, glancing at Madame Delphine, without changing his attitude.

Her answer was to raise her eyes rapturously.

"Which gives us the dilemma in its fullest force," said the priest, speaking as if to the floor. "She has no more place than if she had dropped upon a strange planet." He suddenly looked up with a brightness which almost as quickly passed away, and then he looked down again. His happy thought was the cloister; but he instantly said to himself: "They cannot have overlooked that choice, except intentionally— which they have a right to do." He could do nothing but shake his head.

"And suppose you should suddenly die," he said; he wanted to get at once to the worst.

The woman made a quick gesture, and buried her head in her handkerchief, with the stifled cry:

"Oh, Olive, my daughter!"

"Well, Madame Delphine," said Père Jerome, more buoyantly, "one thing is sure: we *must* find a way out of this trouble."

"Ah!" she exclaimed, looking heavenward, "if it might be!"

"But it must be!" said the priest.

"But how shall it be?" asked the desponding woman.

"Ah!" said Père Jerome, with a shrug, "God knows."

"Yes," said the quadroone, with a quick sparkle in her gentle eye; "and I know, if God would tell anybody, He would tell you!"

The priest smiled and rose.

"Do you think so? Well, leave me to think of it. I will ask Him."

"And He will tell you!" she replied. "And He will bless you!" She rose and gave her hand. As she withdrew it she smiled. "I had such a strange dream," she said, backing toward the door.

"Yes?"

"Yes. I got my troubles all mixed up with your sermon. I dreamed I made that pirate the guardian of my daughter."

Père Jerome smiled also, and shrugged.

"To you, Madame Delphine, as you are placed, every white man in this country, on land or on water, is a pirate, and of all pirates, I think that one is, without doubt, the best."

"Without doubt," echoed Madame Delphine, wearily, still withdrawing backward. Père Jerome stepped forward and opened the door.

The shadow of some one approaching it from without fell upon the threshold, and a man entered, dressed in dark blue cottonade, lifting from his head a fine Panama hat, and from a broad, smooth brow, fair where the hat had covered it, and dark below, gently stroking back his very soft, brown locks. Madame Delphine slightly started aside, while Père Jerome reached silently, but eagerly, forward, grasped a larger hand than his own, and motioned its owner to a seat. Madame Delphine's eyes ventured no higher than to discover that the shoes of the visitor were of white duck.

"Well, Père Jerome," she said, in a hurried undertone, "I am just going to say Hail Marys all the time till you find that out for me!"

"Well, I hope that will be soon, Madame Carraze. Good-day, Madame Carraze."

And as she departed, the priest turned to the newcomer and extended both hands, saying, in the same familiar dialect in which he had been addressing the quadroone :

"Well-a-day, old playmate! After so many years!"

They sat down side by side, like husband and wife, the priest playing with the other's hand, and talked of times and seasons past, often mentioning Evariste and often Jean.

Madame Delphine stopped short half-way home and returned to Père Jerome's. His entry door was wide open and the parlor door ajar. She passed through the one and with downcast eyes was standing at the other, her hand lifted to knock, when the door was drawn open and the white duck shoes passed out. She saw, besides, this time the blue cottonade suit.

"Yes," the voice of Père Jerome was saying, as his face appeared in the door—"Ah! Madame"—

"I lef' my para*sol*," said Madame Delphine, in English.

There was this quiet evidence of a defiant spirit hidden somewhere down under her general timidity, that, against a fierce conventional prohibition, she wore a bonnet instead of the turban of her caste, and carried a parasol.

Père Jerome turned and brought it.

He made a motion in the direction in which the late visitor had disappeared.

"Madame Delphine, you saw dat man?"

"Not his face."

"You couldn' billieve me iv I tell you w'at dat man pur*pose* to do!"

"Is dad so, Père Jerome?"

"He's goin' to hopen a bank!"

"Ah!" said Madame Delphine, seeing she was expected to be astonished.

Père Jerome evidently longed to tell something that was best kept secret; he repressed the impulse, but his heart had to say something. He threw forward one hand and looking pleasantly at Madame Delphine, with his lips dropped apart, clenched his extended hand and thrusting it toward the ground, said in a solemn undertone:

"He is God's own banker, Madame Delphine."

CHAPTER VII.

MICHÉ VIGNEVIELLE.

MADAME DELPHINE sold one of the corner lots of her property. She had almost no revenue, and now and then a piece had to go. As a consequence of the

sale, she had a few large bank-notes sewed up in her
petticoat, and one day — maybe a fortnight after her
tearful interview with Père Jerome — she found it necessary to get one of these changed into small money.
She was in the Rue Toulouse, looking from one side to
the other for a bank which was not in that street at all,
when she noticed a small sign hanging above a door,
bearing the name "Vignevielle." She looked in.
Père Jerome had told her (when she had gone to him
to ask where she should apply for change) that if she
could only wait a few days, there would be a new
concern opened in Toulouse Street, — it really seemed
as if Vignevielle was the name, if she could judge; it
looked to be, and it was, a private banker's, — "U. L.
Vignevielle's," according to a larger inscription which
met her eyes as she ventured in. Behind the counter,
exchanging some last words with a busy-mannered man
outside, who, in withdrawing, seemed bent on running
over Madame Delphine, stood the man in blue cottonade, whom she had met in Père Jerome's doorway.
Now, for the first time, she saw his face, its strong,
grave, human kindness shining softly on each and
every bronzed feature. The recognition was mutual.
He took pains to speak first, saying, in a re-assuring
tone, and in the language he had last heard her use:

"'Ow I kin serve you, Madame?"

"Iv you pliz, to mague dad bill change, Miché."

She pulled from her pocket a wad of dark cotton
handkerchief, from which she began to untie the im-
prisoned note. Madame Delphine had an uncommon-
ly sweet voice, and it seemed so to strike Monsieur

Vignevielle. He spoke to her once or twice more, as he waited on her, each time in English, as though he enjoyed the humble melody of its tone, and presently, as she turned to go, he said:

"Madame Carraze!"

She started a little, but bethought herself instantly that he had heard her name in Père Jerome's parlor. The good father might even have said a few words about her after her first departure; he had such an overflowing heart. "Madame Carraze," said Monsieur Vignevielle, "doze kine of note wad you *an'* me juz now is bein' contrefit. You muz tek kyah from doze kine of note. You see"— He drew from his cash-drawer a note resembling the one he had just changed for her, and proceeded to point out certain tests of genuineness. The counterfeit, he said, was so and so.

"Bud," she exclaimed, with much dismay, "dad was de manner of my bill! Id muz be — led me see dad bill wad I give you, — if you pliz, Miché."

Monsieur Vigneville turned to engage in conversation with an employé and a new visitor, and gave no sign of hearing Madame Delphine's voice. She asked a second time, with like result, lingered timidly, and as he turned to give his attention to a third visitor, reiterated:

"Miché Vignevielle, I wizh you pliz led "—

"Madame Carraze," he said, turning so suddenly as to make the frightened little woman start, but extending his palm with a show of frankness, and assuming a look of benignant patience, "'ow I kin fine doze note now, mongs' all de rez? Iv you p'iz nod to mague me doze troub'."

The dimmest shadow of a smile seemed only to give his words a more kindly authoritative import, and as he turned away again with a manner suggestive of finality, Madame Delphine found no choice but to depart. But she went away loving the ground beneath the feet of Monsieur U. L. Vignevielle.

"Oh, Père Jerome!" she exclaimed in the corrupt French of her caste, meeting the little father on the street a few days later, "you told the truth that day in your parlor. *Mo conné li à c't heure.* I know him now; he is just what you called him."

"Why do you not make him *your* banker, also, Madame Delphine?"

"I have done so this very day!" she replied, with more happiness in her eyes than Père Jerome had ever before seen there.

"Madame Delphine," he said, his own eyes sparkling, "make *him* your daughter's guardian; for myself, being a priest, it would not be best; but ask him; I believe he will not refuse you."

Madame Delphine's face grew still brighter as he spoke.

"It was in my mind," she said.

Yet to the timorous Madame Delphine many trifles became, one after another, an impediment to the making of this proposal, and many weeks elapsed before further delay was positively without excuse. But at length, one day in May, 1822, in a small private office behind Monsieur Vignevielle's banking-room, — he sitting beside a table, and she, more timid and demure than ever, having just taken a chair by the door, — she said,

trying, with a little bashful laugh, to make the matter
seem unimportant, and yet with some tremor of voice:

" Miché Vignevielle, I bin maguing my will." (Having commenced their acquaintance in English, they
spoke nothing else.)

" 'Tis a good idy," responded the banker.

" I kin mague you de troub' to kib dad will fo' me,
Miché Vignevielle?"

" Yez."

She looked up with grateful re-assurance; but her
eyes dropped again as she said:

" Miché Vignevielle" — Here she choked, and began her peculiar motion of laying folds in the skirt
of her dress, with trembling fingers. She lifted her
eyes, and as they met the look of deep and placid kindness that was in his face, some courage returned, and
she said:

" Miché."

" Wad you wand?" asked he, gently.

" If it arrive to me to die " —

" Yez?"

Her words were scarcely audible:

" I wand you teg kyah my lill' girl."

" You 'ave one lill' gal, Madame Carraze?"

She nodded with her face down.

" An' you godd some mo' chillen?"

" No."

" I nevva know dad, Madame Carraze. She's a lill
small gal?"

Mothers forget their daughters' stature. Madame
Delphine said:

" Yez."

For a few moments neither spoke, and then Monsieur Vignevielle said :

"I will do dad."

"Lag she been you' h-own?" asked the mother, suffering from her own boldness.

"She's a good lill' chile, eh?"

"Miché, she's a lill' hangel!" exclaimed Madame Delphine, with a look of distress.

"Yez; I teg kyah 'v 'er, lag my h-own. I mague you dad promise."

"But"— There was something still in the way, Madame Delphine seemed to think.

The banker waited in silence.

"I suppose you will want to see my lill' girl?"

He smiled; for she looked at him as if she would implore him to decline.

"Oh, I tek you' word fo' hall dad, Madame Carraze. It mague no differend wad she loog lag; I don' wan' see 'er."

Madame Delphine's parting smile — she went very shortly — was gratitude beyond speech.

Monsieur Vignevielle returned to the seat he had left, and resumed a newspaper, — the *Louisiana Gazette* in all probability, — which he had laid down upon Madame De.phine's entrance. His eyes fell upon a paragraph which had previously escaped his notice. There they rested. Either he read it over and over unwearyingly, or he was lost in thought. Jean Thompson entered.

"Now," said Mr. Thompson, in a suppressed tone,

bending a little across the table, and laying one palm upon a package of papers which lay in the other, "it is completed. You could retire from your business any day inside of six hours without loss to anybody." (Both here and elsewhere, let it be understood that where good English is given the words were spoken in good French.)

Monsieur Vignevielle raised his eyes and extended the newspaper to the attorney, who received it and read the paragraph. Its substance was that a certain vessel of the navy had returned from a cruise in the Gulf of Mexico and Straits of Florida, where she had done valuable service against the pirates — having, for instance, destroyed in one fortnight in January last twelve pirate vessels afloat, two on the stocks, and three establishments ashore.

"United States brig *Porpoise*," repeated Jean Thompson. "Do you know her?"

"We are acquainted," said Monsieur Vignevielle.

CHAPTER VIII.

SHE.

A QUIET footstep, a grave new presence on financial sidewalks, a neat garb slightly out of date, a gently strong and kindly pensive face, a silent bow, a new sign in the Rue Toulouse, a lone figure with a cane, walking in meditation in the evening light under the

willows of Canal Marigny, a long-darkened window
re-lighted in the Rue Conti — these were all; a fall of
dew would scarce have been more quiet than was the
return of Ursin Lemaitre-Vignevielle to the precincts
of his birth and early life.

But we hardly give the event its right name. It was
Capitaine Lemaitre who had disappeared; it was Monsieur Vignevielle who had come back. The pleasures,
the haunts, the companions, that had once held out
their charms to the impetuous youth, offered no entice-
ments to Madame Delphine's banker. There is this
to be said even for the pride his grandfather had
taught him, that it had always held him above low
indulgences; and though he had dallied with kings,
queens, and knaves through all the mazes of Faro,
Rondeau, and Craps, he had done it loftily; but now
he maintained a peaceful estrangement from all. Evariste and Jean, themselves, found him only by seeking.

"It is the right way," he said to Père Jerome, the
day we saw him there. "Ursin Lemaitre is dead. I
have buried him. He left a will. I am his executor."

"He is crazy," said his lawyer brother-in-law, im-
patiently.

"On the contr-y," replied the little priest, "'e 'as
come ad hisse'f."

Evariste spoke.

"Look at his face, Jean. Men with that kind of
face are the last to go crazy."

"You have not proved that," replied Jean, with an
attorney's obstinacy. "You should have heard him
talk the other day about that newspaper paragraph

' I have taken Ursin Lemaitre's head; I have it with me; I claim the reward, but I desire to commute it to citizenship.' He is crazy."

Of course Jean Thompson did not believe what he said; but he said it, and, in his vexation, repeated it, on the *banquettes* and at the clubs; and presently it took the shape of a sly rumor, that the returned rover was a trifle snarled in his top-hamper.

This whisper was helped into circulation by many trivial eccentricities of manner, and by the unaccountable oddness of some of his transactions in business.

" My dear sir ! " cried his astounded lawyer, one day, " you are not running a charitable institution ! "

" How do you know? " said Monsieur Vignevielle. There the conversation ceased.

" Why do you not found hospitals and asylums at once," asked the attorney, at another time, with a vexed laugh, " and get the credit of it? "

" And make the end worse than the beginning, ' said the banker, with a gentle smile, turning away to a desk of books.

" Bah ! " muttered Jean Thompson.

Monsieur Vignevielle betrayed one very bad symptom. Wherever he went he seemed looking for somebody. It may have been perceptible only to those who were sufficiently interested in him to study his movements; but those who saw it once saw it always. He never passed an open door or gate but he glanced in; and often, where it stood but slightly ajar, you might see him give it a gentle push with his hand or cane It was very singular.

He walked much alone after dark. The *guichinan-goes* (garroters, we might say), at those times the city's particular terror by night, never crossed his path. He was one of those men for whom danger appears to stand aside.

One beautiful summer night, when all nature seemed hushed in ecstasy, the last blush gone that told of the sun's parting, Monsieur Vignevielle, in the course of one of those contemplative, uncompanioned walks which it was his habit to take, came slowly along the more open portion of the Rue Royale, with a step which was soft without intention, occasionally touching the end of his stout cane gently to the ground and looking upward among his old acquaintances, the stars.

It was one of those southern nights under whose spell all the sterner energies of the mind cloak themselves and lie down in bivouac, and the fancy and the imagination, that cannot sleep, slip their fetters and escape, beckoned away from behind every flowering bush and sweet-smelling tree, and every stretch of lonely, half-lighted walk, by the genius of poetry. The air stirred softly now and then, and was still again, as if the breezes lifted their expectant pinions and lowered them once more, awaiting the rising of the moon in a silence which fell upon the fields, the roads, the gardens, the walls, and the suburban and half-suburban streets, like a pause in worship. And anon she rose.

Monsieur Vignevielle's steps were bent toward the more central part of the town, and he was presently passing along a high, close, board-fence, on the right hand side of the way, when, just within this enclosure, and almost overhead, in the dark boughs of a large orange-tree, a mocking-bird began the first low flute-notes of his all-night song. It may have been only the nearness of the songster that attracted the passer's attention, but he paused and looked up.

And then he remarked something more, — that the air where he had stopped was filled with the over-powering sweetness of the night-jasmine. He looked around; it could only be inside the fence. There was a gate just there. Would he push it, as his wont was? The grass was growing about it in a thick turf, as though the entrance had not been used for years. An iron staple clasped the cross-bar, and was driven deep into the gate-post. But now an eye that had been in the blacksmithing business — an eye which had later received high training as an eye for fastenings — fell upon that staple, and saw at a glance that the wood had shrunk from it, and it had sprung from its hold, though without falling out. The strange habit asserted itself; he laid his large hand upon the cross-bar; the turf at the base yielded, and the tall gate was drawn partly open.

At that moment, as at the moment whenever he drew or pushed a door or gate, or looked in at a window, he was thinking of one, the image of whose face and form had never left his inner vision since the day it had met him in his life's path and turned him face about from the way of destruction.

The bird ceased. The cause of the interruption, standing within the opening, saw before him, much

obscured by its own numerous shadows, a broad, ill-
kept, many-flowered garden, among whose untrimmed
rose-trees and tangled vines, and often, also, in its old
walks of pounded shell, the coco-grass and crab-grass
had spread riotously, and sturdy weeds stood up in
bloom. He stepped in and drew the gate to after him.
There, very near by, was the clump of jasmine, whose
ravishing odor had tempted him. It stood just beyond
a brightly moonlit path, which turned from him in a
curve toward the residence, a little distance to the
right, and escaped the view at a point where it seemed
more than likely a door of the house might open upon
it. While he still looked, there fell upon his ear, from
around that curve, a light footstep on the broken shells
—one only, and then all was for a moment still again.
Had he mistaken? No. The same soft click was repeated nearer by, a pale glimpse of robes came through
the tangle, and then, plainly to view, appeared an outline—a presence—a form—a spirit—a girl!

From throat to instep she was as white as Cynthia.
Something above the medium height, slender, lithe, her
abundant hair rolling in dark, rich waves back from
her brows and down from her crown, and falling in
two heavy plaits beyond her round, broadly girt waist
and full to her knees, a few escaping locks eddying
lightly on her graceful neck and her temples,—her
arms, half hid in a snowy mist of sleeve, let down to
guide her spotless skirts free from the dewy touch of
the grass,—straight down the path she came!

Will she stop? Will she turn aside? Will she espy
the dark form in the deep shade of the orange, and,

with one piercing scream, wheel and vanish? She draws near. She approaches the jasmine; she raises her arms, the sleeves falling like a vapor down to the shoulders; rises upon tiptoe, and plucks a spray. O Memory! Can it be? *Can it be?* Is this his quest, or is it lunacy? The ground seems to Monsieur Vigne-vielle the unsteady sea, and he to stand once more on a deck. And she? As she is now, if she but turn toward the orange, the whole glory of the moon will shine upon her face. His heart stands still; he is waiting for her to do that. She reaches up again; this time a bunch for her mother. That neck and throat! Now she fastens a spray in her hair. The mocking-bird cannot withhold; he breaks into song—she turns —she turns her face—it is she, it is she! Madame Delphine's daughter is the girl he met on the ship.

CHAPTER IX.

OLIVE.

She was just passing seventeen — that beautiful year when the heart of the maiden still beats quickly with the surprise of her new dominion, while with gentle dignity her brow accepts the holy coronation of womanhood. The forehead and temples beneath her loosely bound hair were fair without paleness, and meek without languor. She had the soft, lack-lustre beauty of the South; no ruddiness of coral, no waxen

white, no pink of shell; no heavenly blue in the
glance; but a face that seemed, in all its other
beauties, only a tender accompaniment for the large,
brown, melting eyes, where the openness of child-
nature mingled dreamily with the sweet mysteries of
maiden thought. We say no color of shell on face or
throat; but this was no deficiency, that which took its
place being the warm, transparent tint of sculptured
ivory.

This side doorway which led from Madame Delphine's house into her garden was over-arched partly
by an old remnant of vine-covered lattice, and partly
by a crape-myrtle, against whose small, polished trunk
leaned a rustic seat. Here Madame Delphine and
Olive loved to sit when the twilights were balmy or the
moon was bright.

"*Chérie*," said Madame Delphine on one of those
evenings, "why do you dream so much?"

She spoke in the *patois* most natural to her, and
which her daughter had easily learned.

The girl turned her face to her mother, and smiled,
then dropped her glance to the hands in her own lap,
which were listlessly handling the end of a ribbon.
The mother looked at her with fond solicitude. Her
dress was white again; this was but one night since
that in which Monsieur Vignevielle had seen her at the
bush of night-jasmine. He had not been discovered,
but had gone away, shutting the gate, and leaving it
as he had found it.

Her head was uncovered. Its plaited masses, quite
black in the moonlight, hung down and coiled upon

the bench, by her side. Her chaste drapery was of
that revived classic order which the world of fashion
was again laying aside to re-assume the mediæval
bondage of the staylace; for New Orleans was behind
the fashionable world, and Madame Delphine and her
daughter were behind New Orleans. A delicate scarf,
pale blue, of lightly netted worsted, fell from either
shoulder down beside her hands. The look that was
bent upon her changed perforce to one of gentle admiration. She seemed the goddess of the garden.

Olive glanced up. Madame Delphine was not prepared for the movement, and on that account repeated
her question:

"What are you thinking about?"

The dreamer took the hand that was laid upon hers
between her own palms, bowed her head, and gave
them a soft kiss.

The mother submitted. Wherefore, in the silence
which followed, a daughter's conscience felt the burden of having withheld an answer, and Olive presently
said, as the pair sat looking up into the sky:

"I was thinking of Père Jerome's sermon."

Madame Delphine had feared so. Olive had lived on
it ever since the day it was preached. The poor mother
was almost ready to repent having ever afforded her
the opportunity of hearing it. Meat and drink had
become of secondary value to her daughter; she fed
upon the sermon.

Olive felt her mother's thought and knew that her
mother knew her own; but now that she had confessed, she would ask a question:

" Do you think, *maman*, that Père Jerome knows it was I who gave that missal?"

" No," said Madame Delphine, " I am sure he does not."

Another question came more timidly:

" Do — do you think he knows *him?* "

" Yes, I do. He said in his sermon he did."

Both remained for a long time very still, watching the moon gliding in and through among the small dark-and-white clouds. At last the daughter spoke again.

" I wish I was Père — I wish I was as good as Père Jerome."

" My child," said Madame Delphine, her tone betraying a painful summoning of strength to say what she had lacked the courage to utter, — " my child, I pray the good God you will not let your heart go after one whom you may never see in this world! "

The maiden turned her glance, and their eyes met. She cast her arms about her mother's neck, laid her cheek upon it for a moment, and then, feeling the maternal tear, lifted her lips, and, kissing her, said:

" I will not! I will not!"

But the voice was one, not of willing consent, but of desperate resolution.

" It would be useless, anyhow," said the mother, laying her arm around her daughter's waist.

Olive repeated the kiss, prolonging it passionately.

" I have nobody but you," murmured the girl; " I am a poor quadroone! "

She threw back her plaited hair for a third embrace, when a sound in the shrubbery startled them.

" *Qui ci ça ?* " called Madame Delphine, in a frightened voice, as the two stood up, holding to each other.

No answer.

"It was only the dropping of a twig," she whispered, after a long holding of the breath. But they went into the house and barred it everywhere.

It was no longer pleasant to sit up. They retired, and in course of time, but not soon, they fell asleep, holding each other very tight, and fearing, even in their dreams, to hear another twig fall.

CHAPTER X.

BIRDS.

MONSIEUR VIGNEVILLE looked in at no more doors or windows; but if the disappearance of this symptom was a favorable sign, others came to notice which were especially bad, — for instance, wakefulness. At well-nigh any hour of the night, the city guard, which itself dared not patrol singly, would meet him on his slow, unmolested, sky-gazing walk.

"Seems to enjoy it," said Jean Thompson; "the worst sort of evidence. If he showed distress of mind, it would not be so bad; but his calmness, — ugly feature."

The attorney had held his ground so long that he began really to believe it was tenable.

By day, it is true, Monsieur Vignevielle was at his post in his quiet "bank." Yet here, day by day, he was the source of more and more vivid astonishment to those who held preconceived notions of a banker's calling. As a banker, at least, he was certainly out of balance; while as a promenader, it seemed to those who watched him that his ruling idea had now veered about, and that of late he was ever on the quiet alert, not to find, but to evade, somebody.

"Olive, my child," whispered Madame Delphine one morning, as the pair were kneeling side by side on the tiled floor of the church, "yonder is Miché Vignevielle! If you will only look at once — he is just passing a little in — Ah, much too slow again; he stepped out by the side door."

The mother thought it a strange providence that Monsieur Vignevielle should always be disappearing whenever Olive was with her.

One early dawn, Madame Delphine, with a small empty basket on her arm, stepped out upon the *banquette* in front of her house, shut and fastened the door very softly, and stole out in the direction whence you could faintly catch, in the stillness of the daybreak, the songs of the Gascon butchers and the pounding of their meat-axes on the stalls of the distant market-house. She was going to see if she could find some birds for Olive, — the child's appetite was so poor; and, as she was out, she would drop an early prayer at the cathedral. Faith and works.

"One must venture something, sometimes, in the cause of religion," thought she, as she started timorously on her way. But she had not gone a dozen steps before she repented her temerity. There was some one behind her.

There should not be any thing terrible in a footstep merely because it is masculine; but Madame Delphine's mind was not prepared to consider that. A terrible secret was haunting her. Yesterday morning she had found a shoe-track in the garden. She had not disclosed the discovery to Olive, but she had hardly closed her eyes the whole night.

The step behind her now might be the fall of that very shoe. She quickened her pace, but did not leave the sound behind. She hurried forward almost at a run; yet it was still there — no farther, no nearer. Two frights were upon her at once — one for herself, another for Olive, left alone in the house; but she had but the one prayer — " God protect my child ! " After a fearful time she reached a place of safety, the cathedral. There, panting, she knelt long enough to know the pursuit was, at least, suspended, and then arose, hoping and praying all the saints that she might find the way clear for her return in all haste to Olive.

She approached a different door from that by which she had entered, her eyes in all directions and her heart in her throat.

" Madame Carraze."

She started wildly and almost screamed, though the voice was soft and mild. Monsieur Vignevielle came slowly forward from the shade of the wall. They met beside a bench, upon which she dropped her basket.

"Ah, Miché Vignevielle, I thang de good God to mid you!"

"Is dad so, Madame Carraze? Fo' w'y dad is?"

"A man was chase me all dad way since my 'ouse!"

"Yes, Madame, I sawed him."

"You sawed 'im? Oo it was?"

"'Twas only one man wad is a foolizh. De people say he's crezzie. *Mais*, he don' goin' to meg you no 'arm."

"But I was scare' fo' my lill' girl."

"Noboddie don' goin' trouble you' lill' gal, Madame Carraze."

Madame Delphine looked up into the speaker's strangely kind and patient eyes, and drew sweet reassurance from them.

"Madame," said Monsieur Vignevielle, "wad pud you hout so hearly dis morning?"

She told him her errand. She asked if he thought she would find any thing.

"Yez," he said, "it was possible — a few lill' *bécassines-de-mer*, ou somezin' ligue. But fo' w'y you lill' gal lose doze hapetide?"

"Ah, Miché," — Madame Delphine might have tried a thousand times again without ever succeeding half so well in lifting the curtain upon the whole, sweet, tender, old, old-fashioned truth, — "Ah, Miché, she wone tell me!"

"Bud, anny'ow, Madame, wad you thing?"

"Miché," she replied, looking up again with a tear standing in either eye, and then looking down once more as she began to speak, "I thing — I thing she's lonesome."

" You thing? "

She nodded.

" Ah! Madame Carraze," he said, partly extending his hand, " you see? 'Tis impossible to mague you' owze shud so tighd to priv-en dad. Madame, I med one mizteg."

" Ah, *non*, Miché ! "

" Yez. There har nod one poss'bil'ty fo' me to be dad guardian of you' daughteh ! "

Madame Delphine started with surprise and alarm.

" There is ondly one wad can be," he continued.

" But oo, Miché? "

" God."

" Ah, Miché Vignevielle " — She looked at him appealingly.

" I don' goin' to dizzerd you, Madame Carraze," he said.

She lifted her eyes. They filled. She shook her head, a tear fell, she bit her lip, smiled, and suddenly dropped her face into both hands, sat down upon the bench and wept until she shook.

" You dunno wad I mean, Madame Carraze? "

She did not know.

" I mean dad guardian of you' daughteh godd to fine 'er now one 'uzhan'; an' noboddie are hable to do dad egceb de good God 'imsev. But, Madame, I tell you wad I do."

She rose up. He continued:

" Go h-open you' owze; I fin' you' daughteh dad uzban'."

Madame Delphine was a helpless, timid thing; but

her eyes showed she was about to resent this offer.
Monsieur Vignevielle put forth his hand — it touched
her shoulder — and said, kindly still, and without
eagerness :

"One w'ite man, Madame : 'tis prattycabble. I
know 'tis prattycabble. One w'ite jantleman, Madame.
You can truz me. I goin' fedge 'im. H-ondly you
go h-open you' owze."

Madame Delphine looked down, twining her handkerchief among her fingers.

He repeated his proposition.

"You will come firz by you'se'f ? " she asked.

"Iv you wand."

She lifted up once more her eye of faith. That was
her answer.

"Come," he said, gently, "I wan' sen' some biri
ad you' lill' gal."

And they went away, Madame Delphine's spirit
grown so exaltedly bold that she said as they went,
though a violent blush followed her words :

"Miché Vignevielle, I thing Père Jerome mighd be
ab'e to tell you someboddie."

CHAPTER XI.

FACE TO FACE.

MADAME DELPHINE found her house neither burned
nor rifled.

"*Ah ! ma piti sans popa !* Ah ! my little fatherless

one!" Her faded bonnet fell back between her shoulders, hanging on by the strings, and her dropped basket, with its "few lill' *bécassines-de-mer*" dangling from the handle, rolled out its okra and soup-joint upon the floor. "*Ma piti!* kiss!—kiss!—kiss!"

"But is it good news you have, or bad?" cried the girl, a fourth or fifth time.

"*Dieu sait, ma cère; mo pas conné!*"—God knows, my darling; I cannot tell!

The mother dropped into a chair, covered her face with her apron, and burst into tears, then looked up with an effort to smile, and wept afresh.

"What have you been doing?" asked the daughter, in a long-drawn, fondling tone. She leaned forward and unfastened her mother's bonnet-strings. "Why do you cry?"

"For nothing at all, my darling; for nothing—I am such a fool."

The girl's eyes filled. The mother looked up into her face and said:

"No, it is nothing, nothing, only that"—turning her head from side to side with a slow, emotional emphasis, "Miché Vignevielle is the best—*best* man on the good Lord's earth!"

Olive drew a chair close to her mother, sat down and took the little yellow hands into her own white lap, and looked tenderly into her eyes. Madame Delphine felt herself yielding; she must make a show of telling something:

"He sent you those birds!"

The girl drew her face back a little. The little

woman turned away, trying in vain to hide her tearful smile, and they laughed together, Olive mingling a daughter's fond kiss with her laughter.

"There is something else," she said, "and you shall tell me."

"Yes," replied Madame Delphine, "only let me get composed."

But she did not get so. Later in the morning she came to Olive with the timid yet startling proposal that they would do what they could to brighten up the long-neglected front room. Olive was mystified and troubled, but consented, and thereupon the mother's spirits rose.

The work began, and presently ensued all the thumping, the trundling, the lifting and letting down, the raising and swallowing of dust, and the smells of turpentine, brass, pumice and woollen rags that go to characterize a housekeeper's *émeute;* and still, as the work progressed, Madame Delphine's heart grew light, and her little black eyes sparkled.

"We like a clean parlor, my daughter, even though no one is ever coming to see us, eh?" she said, as entering the apartment she at last sat down, late in the afternoon. She had put on her best attire.

Olive was not there to reply. The mother called but got no answer. She rose with an uneasy heart, and met her a few steps beyond the door that opened into the garden, in a path which came up from an old latticed bower. Olive was approaching slowly, her face pale and wild. There was an agony of hostile dismay in the look. and the trembling and appealing tone with which, taking the frightened mother's cheeks between her palms, she said :

"*Ah! ma mère, qui vini 'ci ce soir?*"—Who is coming here this evening?

"Why, my dear child, I was just saying, we like a clean"—

But the daughter was desperate :

"Oh, tell me, my mother, *who* is coming?"

"My darling, it is our blessed friend, Miché Vigne-vielle!"

"To see me?" cried the girl.

"Yes."

"Oh, my mother, what have you done?"

"Why, Olive, my child," exclaimed the little mother, bursting into tears, "do you forget it is Miché Vigne-vielle who has promised to protect you when I die?"

The daughter had turned away, and entered the door; but she faced around again, and extending her arms toward her mother, cried :

"How can—he is a white man—I am a poor"—

"Ah! *chérie*," replied Madame Delphine, seizing the outstretched hands, "it is there—it is there that he shows himself the best man alive! He sees that difficulty; he proposes to meet it; he says he will find you a suitor!"

Olive freed her hands violently, motioned her mother back, and stood proudly drawn up, flashing an indignation too great for speech; but the next moment she had uttered a cry, and was sobbing on the floor.

The mother knelt beside her and threw an arm about her shoulders.

"Oh, my sweet daughter, you must not cry! I did not want to tell you at all! I did not want to tell you! It isn't fair for you to cry so hard. Miché Vignevielle says you shall have the one you wish, or none at all, Olive, or none at all."

"None at all! none at all! None, none, none!"

"No, no, Olive," said the mother, "none at all. He brings none with him to-night, and shall bring none with him hereafter."

Olive rose suddenly, silently declined her mother's aid, and went alone to their chamber in the half-story.

Madame Delphine wandered drearily from door to window, from window to door, and presently into the newly-furnished front room which now seemed dismal beyond degree. There was a great Argand lamp in one corner. How she had labored that day to prepare it for evening illumination! A little beyond it, on the wall, hung a crucifix. She knelt under it, with her eyes fixed upon it, and thus silently remained until its outline was indistinguishable in the deepening shadows of evening.

She arose. A few minutes later, as she was trying to light the lamp, an approaching step on the sidewalk seemed to pause. Her heart stood still. She softly laid the phosphorus-box out of her hands. A shoe grated softly on the stone step, and Madame Delphine, her heart beating in great thuds, without waiting for a knock, opened the door, bowed low, and exclaimed in a soft perturbed voice:

"Miché Vignevielle!"

He entered, hat in hand, and with that almost noise-
.ess tread which we have noticed. She gave him a
chair and closed the door; then hastened, with words
of apology, back to her task of lighting the lamp.
But her hands paused in their work again, — Olive's
step was on the stairs; then it came off the stairs;
then it was in the next room, and then there was the
whisper of soft robes, a breath of gentle perfume, and
a snowy figure in the door. She was dressed for the
evening.

" Maman ? "

Madame Delphine was struggling desperately with
the lamp, and at that moment it responded with a tiny
bead of light.

" I am here, my daughter."

She hastened to the door, and Olive, all unaware of
a third presence, lifted her white arms, laid them about
her mother's neck, and, ignoring her effort to speak,
wrested a fervent kiss from her lips. The crystal of
the lamp sent out a faint gleam; it grew; it spread on
every side; the ceiling, the walls lighted up; the crucifix, the furniture of the room came back into shape.

" Maman ! " cried Olive, with a tremor of conster-
nation.

" It is Miché Vignevielle, my daughter " —

The gloom melted swiftly away before the eyes of
the startled maiden, a dark form stood out against the
farther wall, and the light, expanding to the full, shone
clearly upon the unmoving figure and quiet face of
Capitaine Lemaitre.

CHAPTER XII.

THE MOTHER BIRD.

ONE afternoon, some three weeks after Capitaine
Lemaitre had called on Madame Delphine, the priest
started to make a pastoral call and had hardly left the
gate of his cottage, when a person, overtaking him,
plucked his gown:

"Père Jerome" —

He turned.

The face that met his was so changed with excitement and distress that for an instant he did not rec-
ognize it.

"Why, Madame Delphine" —

"Oh, Père Jerome! I wan' see you so bad, so
bad! *Mo oulé dit quiç'ose,* — I godd some' to tell
you."

The two languages might be more successful than
one, she seemed to think.

"We had better go back to my parlor," said the
priest, in their native tongue.

They returned.

Madame Delphine's very step was altered, — nervous and inelastic. She swung one arm as she walked,
and brandished a turkey-tail fan.

"I was glad, yass, to kedge you," she said, as
they mounted the front, outdoor stair; following her
speech with a slight, unmusical laugh, and fanning
herself with unconscious fury.

"*Fé chaud,*" she remarked again, taking the chair he offered and continuing to ply the fan.

Père Jerome laid his hat upon a chest of drawers, sat down opposite her, and said, as he wiped his kindly face:

"Well, Madame Carraze?"

Gentle as the tone was, she started, ceased fanning, lowered the fan to her knee, and commenced smoothing its feathers.

"Père Jerome" — She gnawed her lip and shook her head.

"Well?"

She burst into tears.

The priest rose and loosed the curtain of one of the windows. He did it slowly — as slowly as he could, and, as he came back, she lifted her face with sudden energy, and exclaimed:

"Oh, Père Jerome, de law is brogue! de law is brogue! I brogue it! 'Twas me! 'Twas me!"

The tears gushed out again, but she shut her lips very tight, and dumbly turned away her face. Père Jerome waited a little before replying; then he said, very gently:

"I suppose dad muss 'ave been by accyden', Madame Delphine?"

The little father felt a wish — one which he often had when weeping women were before him — that he were an angel instead of a man, long enough to press the tearful cheek upon his breast, and assure the weeper God would not let the lawyers and judges hurt her. He allowed a few moments more to pass, and then asked:

"*N'est-ce-pas*, Madame Delphine? Dez ze way, ain't it?"

"No, Père Jerome, no. My daughter — oh, Père Jerome, I bethroath my lill' girl — to a w'ite man!" And immediately Madame Delphine commenced savagely drawing a thread in the fabric of her skirt with one trembling hand, while she drove the fan with the other. "Dey goin' git marry."

On the priest's face came a look of pained surprise. He slowly said:

"Is dad possib', Madame Delphine?"

"Yass," she replied, at first without lifting her eyes; and then again, "Yass," looking full upon him through her tears, "yaas, 'tis tru'."

He rose and walked once across the room, returned, and said, in the Creole dialect:

"Is he a good man — withort doubt?"

"De bez in God's world!" replied Madame Delphine, with a rapturous smile.

"My poor, dear friend," said the priest, "I am afraid you are being deceived by somebody."

There was the pride of an unswerving faith in the triumphant tone and smile with which she replied, raising and slowly shaking her head:

"Ah-h, no-o-o, Miché! Ah-h, no, no! Not by Ursin Lemaitre-Vignevielle!"

Père Jerome was confounded. He turned again, and, with his hands at his back and his eyes cast down, slowly paced the floor.

"He *is* a good man," he said, by and by, as if he thought aloud. At length he halted before the woman

" Madame Delphine " —

The distressed glance with which she had been fol
owing his steps was lifted to his eyes.

"Suppose dad should be true w'at doze peop' say
'bout Ursin."

"*Qui ci ça ?* What is that?" asked the quadroone,
stopping her fan.

"Some peop' say Ursin is crezzie."

" Ah, Père Jerome ! " She leaped to her feet as if
he had smitten her, and putting his words away with
an outstretched arm and wide-open palm, suddenly
lifted hands and eyes to heaven, and cried : " I wizh
to God — *I wizh to God* — de whole worl' was crezzie
dad same way ! " She sank, trembling, into her chair.
" Oh, no, no," she continued, shaking her head, " 'tis
not Miché Vignevielle w'at's crezzie." Her eyes
lighted with sudden fierceness. " 'Tis dad *law !* Dad
law is crezzie ! Dad law is a fool ! "

A priest of less heart-wisdom might have replied
that the law is — the law ; but Père Jerome saw that
Madame Delphine was expecting this very response.
Wherefore he said, with gentleness :

" Madame Delphine, a priest is not a bailiff, but a
physician. How can I help you?"

A grateful light shone a moment in her eyes, yet
there remained a piteous hostility in the tone in which
she demanded :

" *Mais, pou'quoi yé fé cette méchanique là ?*" — What
business had they to make that contraption?

His answer was a shrug with his palms extended
and a short, disclamatory " Ah." He started to re-
sume his walk, but turned to her again and said :

"Why did they make that law? Well, they made it to keep the two races separate."

Madame Delphine startled the speaker with a loud, harsh, angry laugh. Fire came from her eyes and her lip curled with scorn.

"Then they made a lie, Père Jerome! Separate! No-o-o! They do not want to keep us separated; no, no! But they *do* want to keep us despised!" She laid her hand on her heart, and frowned upward with physical pain. "But, very well! from which race do they want to keep my daughter separate? She is seven parts white! The law did not stop her from being that; and now, when she wants to be a white man's good and honest wife, shall that law stop her? Oh, no!" She rose up. "No; I will tell you what that law is made for. It is made to — punish — my — child — for — not — choosing — her — father! Père Jerome — my God, what a law!" She dropped back into her seat. The tears came in a flood, which she made no attempt to restrain.

"No," she began again — and here she broke into English — "fo' me I don' kyare; but, Père Jerome, — 'tis fo' dat I came to tell you, — dey *shall not* punizh my daughter!" She was on her feet again, smiting her heaving bosom with the fan. "She shall marrie oo she want!"

Pére Jerome had heard her out, not interrupting by so much as a motion of the hand. Now his decision was made, and he touched her softly with the ends of his fingers.

"Madame Delphine, I want you to go at 'ome. Go at 'ome."

" Wad you goin' mague ? " she asked.

" Nottin'. But go at 'ome. Kip quite ; don put you'se'f sig. I goin' see Ursin. We trah to figs dat .aw fo' you."

" You kin figs dad ! " she cried, with a gleam of joy.

" We goin' to try, Madame Delphine. Adieu ! "

He offered his hand. She seized and kissed it thrice, covering it with tears, at the same time lifting up her eyes to his and murmuring :

" De bez man God evva mague ! "

At the door she turned to offer a more conventional good-by ; but he was following her out, bareheaded. At the gate they paused an instant, and then parted with a simple adieu, she going home and he returning for his hat, and starting again upon his interrupted business.

Before he came back to his own house, he stopped at the lodgings of Monsieur Vignevielle, but did not find him in.

" Indeed," the servant at the door said, " he said he might not return for some days or weeks."

So Père Jerome, much wondering, made a second detour toward the residence of one of Monsieur Vignevielle's employés.

" Yes," said the clerk, " his instructions are to hold the business, as far as practicable, in suspense, during his absence. Every thing is in another name." And then he whispered :

" Officers of the Government looking for him. In-

formation get from some of the prisoners taken months
ago by the United States brig *Porpoise*. But " — a
still softer whisper — " have no fear ; they will nevei
find him : Jean Thompson and Evariste Varrillat have
hid him away too well for that."

CHAPTER XIII.

TRIBULATION.

THE Saturday following was a very beautiful day.
In the morning a light fall of rain had passed across
the town, and all the afternoon you could see signs,
here and there upon the horizon, of other showers.
The ground was dry again, while the breeze was cool
and sweet, smelling of wet foliage and bringing sunshine and shade in frequent and very pleasing alterna-
tion.

There was a walk in Père Jerome's little garden, of
which we have not spoken, off on the right side of the
cottage, with his chamber window at one end, a few
old and twisted, but blossom-laden, crape-myrtles on
either hand, now and then a rose of some unpretending
variety and some bunches of rue, and at the other end
a shrine, in whose blue niche stood a small figure of
Mary, with folded hands and uplifted eyes.   No other
window looked down upon the spot, and its seclusion
was often a great comfort to Père Jerome.

Up and down this path, but a few steps in its entire

length, the priest was walking, taking the air for a few moments after a prolonged sitting in the confessional. Penitents had been numerous this afternoon. He was thinking of Ursin. The officers of the Government had not found him, nor had Père Jerome seen him; yet he believed they had, in a certain indirect way, devised a simple project by which they could at any time "figs dad law," providing only that these Government officials would give over their search; for, though he had not seen the fugitive, Madame Delphine had seen him, and had been the vehicle of communication between them. There was an orange-tree, where a mocking-bird was wont to sing and a girl in white to walk, that the detectives wot not of. The law was to be "figs" by the departure of the three frequenters of the jasmine-scented garden in one ship to France, where the law offered no obstacles.

It seemed moderately certain to those in search of Monsieur Vignevielle (and it was true) that Jean and Evariste were his harborers; but for all that the hunt, even for clews, was vain. The little banking establishment had not been disturbed. Jean Thompson had told the searchers certain facts about it, and about its gentle proprietor as well, that persuaded them to make no move against the concern, if the same relations did not even induce a relaxation of their efforts for his personal discovery.

Père Jerome was walking to and fro, with his hands behind him, pondering these matters. He had paused a moment at the end of the walk farthest from his window, and was looking around upon the sky, when, turn-

ing, he beheld a closely veiled female figure standing
at the other end, and knew instantly that it was Olive.

She came forward quickly and with evident eagerness.

"I came to confession," she said, breathing hurriedly, the excitement in her eyes shining through her
veil, "but I find I am too late."

"There is no too late or too early for that; I am
always ready," said the priest. "But how is your
mother?"

"Ah!" —

Her voice failed.

"More trouble?"

"Ah, sir, I have *made* trouble. Oh, Père Jerome,
I am bringing so much trouble upon my poor mother!"

Père Jerome moved slowly toward the house, with
his eyes cast down, the veiled girl at his side.

"It is not your fault," he presently said. And
after another pause: "I thought it was all arranged."

He looked up and could see, even through the veil,
her crimson blush.

"Oh, no," she replied, in a low, despairing voice,
dropping her face.

"What is the difficulty?" asked the priest, stopping
in the angle of the path, where it turned toward the
front of the house.

She averted her face, and began picking the thin
scales of bark from a crape-myrtle.

"Madame Thompson and her husband were at our
house this morning. *He* had told Monsieur Thompson
all about it. They were very kind to me at first, but
they tried" — She was weeping.

"What did they try to do?" asked the priest.

"They tried to make me believe he is insane."

She succeeded in passing her handkerchief up under her veil.

"And I suppose then your poor mother grew angry, eh?"

"Yes; and they became much more so, and said if we did not write, or send a writing, to *him*, within twenty-four hours, breaking the" —

"Engagement," said Père Jerome.

"They would give him up to the Government. Oh, Père Jerome, what shall I do? It is killing my mother!"

She bowed her head and sobbed.

"Where is your mother now?"

"She has gone to see Monsieur Jean Thompson. She says she has a plan that will match them all. I do not know what it is. I begged her not to go; but oh, sir, *she is* crazy, — and I am no better."

"My poor child," said Père Jerome, "what you seem to want is not absolution, but relief from persecution."

"Oh, father, I have committed mortal sin, — I am guilty of pride and anger."

"Nevertheless," said the priest, starting toward his front gate, "we will put off your confession. Let it go until to-morrow morning; you will find me in my box just before mass; I will hear you then. My child, I know that in your heart, now, you begrudge the time it would take; and that is right. There are moments when we are not in place even on penitential knees.

It is so with you now. We must find your mother Go you at once to your house; if she is there, comfort her as best you can, and *keep her in, if possible,* until I come. If she is not there, stay; leave me to find her; one of you, at least, must be where I can get word to you promptly. God comfort and uphold you. I hope you may find her at home; tell her, for me, not to fear," — he lifted the gate-latch, — "that she and her daughter are of more value than many sparrows; that God's priest sends her that word from Him. Tell her to fix her trust in the great Husband of the Church and she shall yet see her child receiving the grace-giving sacrament of matrimony. Go; I shall, in a few minutes, be on my way to Jean Thompson's, and shall find her, either there or wherever she is. Go; they shall not oppress you. Adieu!"

A moment or two later he was in the street himself.

CHAPTER XIV.

BY AN OATH.

Père Jerome, pausing on a street-corner in the last hour of sunlight, had wiped his brow and taken his cane down from under his arm to start again, when somebody, coming noiselessly from he knew not where, asked, so suddenly as to startle him:

"*Miché, commin yé pellé la rie ici ?* — how do they call this street here?"

It was by the bonnet and dress, disordered though they were, rather than by the haggard face which looked distractedly around, that he recognized the woman to whom he replied in her own *patois:*

"It is the Rue Burgundy. Where are you going, Madame Delphine?"

She almost leaped from the ground.

"Oh, Père Jerome! *mo pas conné,*—I dunno. You know w'ere's dad 'ouse of Miché Jean Tomkin? *Mo courri 'ci, mo courri là,*—*mo pas capabe li trouvé.* I go (run) here—there—I cannot find it," she gesticulated.

"I am going there myself," said he; "but why do you want to see Jean Thompson, Madame Delphine?"

"I *'blige'* to see 'im!" she replied, jerking herself half around away, one foot planted forward with an air of excited pre-occupation; "I godd some' to tell 'im wad I *'blige'* to tell 'im!"

"Madame Delphine"—

"Oh! Père Jerome, fo' de love of de good God, show me dad way to de 'ouse of Jean Tomkin!"

Her distressed smile implored pardon for her rudeness.

"What are you going to tell him?" asked the priest.

"Oh, Père Jerome,"—in the Creole *patois* again,—"I am going to put an end to all this trouble—only I pray you do not ask me about it now; every minute is precious!"

He could not withstand her look of entreaty.

"Come," he said, and they went.

Jean Thompson and Doctor Varrillat lived opposite

each other on the Bayou road, a little way beyond the
town limits as then prescribed. Each had his large,
white-columned, four-sided house among the magnolias,—his huge live-oak overshadowing either corner of
the darkly shaded garden, his broad, brick walk leading down to the tall, brick-pillared gate, his square of
bright, red pavement on the turf-covered sidewalk, and
his railed platform spanning the draining-ditch, with
a pair of green benches, one on each edge, facing each
other crosswise of the gutter. There, any sunset hour,
you were sure to find the householder sitting beside
his cool-robed matron, two or three slave nurses in
white turbans standing at hand, and an excited throng
of fair children, nearly all of a size.

Sometimes, at a beckon or call, the parents on one
side of the way would join those on the other, and the
children and nurses of both families would be given
the liberty of the opposite platform and an ice-cream
fund! Generally the parents chose the Thompson
platform, its outlook being more toward the sunset.

Such happened to be the arrangement this afternoon.
The two husbands sat on one bench and their wives on
the other, both pairs very quiet, waiting respectfully
for the day to die, and exchanging only occasional
comments on matters of light moment as they passed
through the memory. During one term of silence
Madame Varrillat, a pale, thin-faced, but cheerful-
looking lady, touched Madame Thompson, a person of
two and a half times her weight, on her extensive and
snowy bare elbow, directing her attention obliquely
up and across the road.

About a hundred yards distant, in the direction of the river, was a long, pleasantly shaded green strip of turf, destined in time for a sidewalk. It had a deep ditch on the nearer side, and a fence of rough cypress palisades on the farther, and these were overhung, on the one hand, by a row of bitter-orange-trees inside the enclosure, and, on the other, by a line of slanting china-trees along the outer edge of the ditch. Down this cool avenue two figures were approaching side by side. They had first attracted Madame Varrillat's notice by the bright play of sunbeams which, as they walked, fell upon them in soft, golden flashes through the chinks between the palisades.

Madame Thompson elevated a pair of glasses which were no detraction from her very good looks, and remarked, with the serenity of a reconnoitring general:

"*Père Jerome et cette milatraise.*"

All eyes were bent toward them.

"She walks like a man," said Madame Varrillat, in the language with which the conversation had opened.

"No," said the physician, "like a woman in a state of high nervous excitement."

Jean Thompson kept his eyes on the woman, and said:

"She must not forget to walk like a woman in the State of Louisiana," — as near as the pun can be translated. The company laughed. Jean Thompson looked at his wife, whose applause he prized, and she answered by an asseverative toss of the head, leaning back and contriving, with some effort, to get her arms folded. Her laugh was musical and low, but enough to make the folded arms shake gently up and down.

"Père Jerome is talking to her," said one. The priest was at that moment endeavoring, in the interest of peace, to say a good word for the four people who sat watching his approach. It was in the old strain :

"Blame them one part, Madame Delphine, and their fathers, mothers, brothers, and fellow-citizens the other ninety-nine."

But to every thing she had the one amiable answer which Père Jerome ignored :

"I am going to arrange it to satisfy everybody, all together. *Tout à fait.*"

"They are coming here," said Madame Varrillat, half articulately.

"Well, of course," murmured another; and the four rose up, smiling courteously, the doctor and attorney advancing and shaking hands with the priest.

No — Père Jerome thanked them — he could not sit down.

"This, I believe you know, Jean, is Madame Delphine " —

The quadroone courtesied.

"A friend of mine," he added, smiling kindly upon her, and turning, with something imperative in his eye, to the group. "She says she has an important private matter to communicate."

"To me?" asked Jean Thompson.

"To all of you ; so I will — Good-evening." He responded nothing to the expressions of regret. but turned to Madame Delphine. She murmured something.

"Ah ! yes, certainly." He addressed the company

' She wishes me to speak for her veracity; it is unimpeachable. Well, good-evening.'' He shook hands and departed.

The four resumed their seats, and turned their eyes upon the standing figure.

'' Have you something to say to us?'' asked Jean Thompson, frowning at her law-defying bonnet.

'' Oui,'' replied the woman, shrinking to one side, and laying hold of one of the benches, '' *mo oulé di' tou' ç'ose* '' — I want to tell every thing. '' *Miché Vignevielle la plis bon homme di moune* '' — the best man in the world; '' *mo pas capabe li fé tracas* '' — I cannot give him trouble. '' *Mo pas capabe, non; m'olé di' tous ç'ose.* '' She attempted to fan herself, her face turned away from the attorney, and her eyes rested on the ground.

'' Take a seat,'' said Doctor Varrillat, with some suddenness, starting from his place and gently guiding her sinking form into the corner of the bench. The ladies rose up; somebody had to stand; the two races could not both sit down at once — at least not in that public manner.

'' Your salts,'' said the physician to his wife. She handed the vial. Madame Delphine stood up again.

'' We will all go inside,'' said Madame Thompson, and they passed through the gate and up the walk, mounted the steps, and entered the deep, cool drawing-room.

Madame Thompson herself bade the quadroone be seated.

'' Well?'' said Jean Thompson, as the rest took chairs.

"*C'est drole*" — it's funny—said Madame Delphine, with a piteous effort to smile, "that nobody thought of it. It is so plain. You have only to look and see. I mean about Olive." She loosed a button in the front of her dress and passed her hand into her bosom. "And yet, Olive herself never thought of it. She does not know a word."

The hand came out holding a miniature. Madame Varrillat passed it to Jean Thompson.

"*Ouala so popa*," said Madame Delphine. "That is her father."

It went from one to another, exciting admiration and murmured praise.

"She is the image of him," said Madame Thompson, in an austere undertone, returning it to her husband.

Doctor Varrillat was watching Madame Delphine. She was very pale. She had passed a trembling hand into a pocket of her skirt, and now drew out another picture, in a case the counterpart of the first. He reached out for it, and she handed it to him. He looked at it a moment, when his eyes suddenly lighted up and he passed it to the attorney.

"*Et là*"—Madame Delphine's utterance failed—"*et là ouala sa moman.* That is her mother."

The three others instantly gathered around Jean Thompson's chair. They were much impressed.

"It is true beyond a doubt!" muttered Madame Thompson.

Madame Varrillat looked at her with astonishment.

"The proof is right there in the faces," said Madame Thompson.

"Yes! yes!" said Madame Delphine, excitedly; "the proof is there! You do not want any better! I am willing to swear to it! But you want no better proof! That is all anybody could want! My God! you cannot help but see it!"

Her manner was wild.

Jean Thompson looked at her sternly.

"Nevertheless you say you are willing to take your solemn oath to this."

"Certainly" —

"You will have to do it."

"Certainly, Miché Thompson, *of course* I shall; you will make out the paper and I will swear before God that it is true! Only "—turning to the ladies—"do not tell Olive; she will never believe it. It will break her heart! It "—

A servant came and spoke privately to Madame Thompson, who rose quickly and went to the hall. Madame Delphine continued, rising unconsciously:

"You see, I have had her with me from a baby. She knows no better. He brought her to me only two months old. Her mother had died in the ship, coming out here. He did not come straight from home here. His people never knew he was married!"

The speaker looked around suddenly with a startled glance. There was a noise of excited speaking in the hall.

"It is not true, Madame Thompson!" cried a girl's voice.

Madame Delphine's look became one of wildest distress and alarm, and she opened her lips in a vain attempt to utter some request, when Olive appeared a moment in the door, and then flew into her arms.

"My mother! my mother! my mother!"

Madame Thompson, with tears in her eyes, tenderly drew them apart and let Madame Delphine down into her chair, while Olive threw herself upon her knees, continuing to cry:

"Oh, my mother! Say you are my mother!"

Madame Delphine looked an instant into the upturned face, and then turned her own away, with a long, low cry of pain, looked again, and laying both hands upon the suppliant's head, said:

"*Oh, chère piti à moin, to pa' ma fie!*" — Oh, my darling little one, you are not my daughter! — Her eyes closed, and her head sank back; the two gentlemen sprang to her assistance, and laid her upon a sofa unconscious.

When they brought her to herself, Olive was kneeling at her head silently weeping.

"*Maman, chère maman!*" said the girl softly, kissing her lips.

"*Ma courri c'ez moin*" — I will go home — said the mother, drearily.

"You will go home with me," said Madame Varrillat, with great kindness of manner — "just across the street here; I will take care of you till you feel better. And Olive will stay here with Madame Thompson. You will be only the width of the street apart."

But Madame Delphine would go nowhere but to her home. Olive she would not allow to go with her.

Then they wanted to send a servant or two to sleep in the house with her for aid and protection; but all she would accept was the transient service of a messenger to invite two of her kinspeople — man and wife — to come and make their dwelling with her.

In course of time these two — a poor, timid, helpless pair — fell heir to the premises. Their children had it after them; but, whether in those hands or these, the house had its habits and continued in them; and to this day the neighbors, as has already been said, rightly explain its close-sealed, uninhabited look by the all-sufficient statement that the inmates "is quadroons."

CHAPTER XV.

KYRIE ELEISON.

THE second Saturday afternoon following was hot and calm. The lamp burning before the tabernacle in Père Jerome's little church might have hung with as motionless a flame in the window behind. The lilies of St. Joseph's wand, shining in one of the half opened panes, were not more completely at rest than the leaves on tree and vine without, suspended in the slumbering air. Almost as still, down under the organ-gallery, with a single band of light falling athwart his box from a small door which stood ajar, sat the little priest, behind the lattice of the confessional, silently wiping away the sweat that beaded on

his brow and rolled down his face. At distant inter
vals the shadow of some one entering softly through
the door would obscure, for a moment, the band of
light, and an aged crone, or a little boy, or some gentle presence that the listening confessor had known
only by the voice for many years, would kneel a few
moments beside his waiting ear, in prayer for blessing
and in review of those slips and errors which prove us
all akin.

The day had been long and fatiguing. First, early
mass; a hasty meal; then a business call upon the
archbishop in the interest of some projected charity;
then back to his cottage, and so to the banking-house
of "Vignevielle," in the Rue Toulouse.   There all
was open, bright, and re-assured, its master virtually,
though not actually, present. The search was over
and the seekers gone, personally wiser than they would
tell, and officially reporting that (to the best of their
knowledge and belief, based on evidence, and especially
on the assurances of an unexceptionable eye-witness,
to wit, Monsieur Vignevielle, banker) Capitaine Lemaitre was dead and buried. At noon there had been
a wedding in the little church. Its scenes lingered before Père Jerome's vision now — the kneeling pair:
the bridegroom, rich in all the excellences of man,
strength and kindness slumbering interlocked in every
part and feature; the bride, a saintly weariness on her
pale face, her awesome eyes lifted in adoration upon
the image of the Saviour; the small knots of friends
behind: Madame Thompson, large, fair, self-contained;
Jean Thompson, with the affidavit of Madame Delphine

showing through his tightly buttoned coat; the physician and his wife, sharing one expression of amiable
consent; and last — yet first — one small, shrinking
female figure, here at one side, in faded robes and
dingy bonnet. She sat as motionless as stone, yet
wore a look of apprehension, and in the small, restless
black eyes which peered out from the pinched and
wasted face, betrayed the peacelessness of a harrowed
mind; and neither the recollection of bride, nor of
groom, nor of potential friends behind, nor the occupation of the present hour, could shut out from the
tired priest the image of that woman, or the sound of
his own low words of invitation to her, given as the
company left the church — "Come to confession this
afternoon."

By and by a long time passed without the approach
of any step, or any glancing of light or shadow, save
for the occasional progress from station to station of
some one over on the right who was noiselessly going
the way of the cross. Yet Père Jerome tarried.

"She will surely come," he said to himself; "she
promised she would come."

A moment later, his sense, quickened by the prolonged silence, caught a subtle evidence or two of
approach, and the next moment a penitent knelt noiselessly at the window of his box, and the whisper came
tremblingly, in the voice he had waited to hear:

"*Bénissez-moin, mo' Père, pa'ce que mo péché.*"
(Bless me, father, for I have sinned.)

He gave his blessing.

"*Ainsi soit-il* — Amen," murmured the penitent,

and then, in the soft accents of the Creole *patois*, continued:

"'I confess to Almighty God, to the blessed Mary, ever Virgin, to blessed Michael the Archangel, to blessed John the Baptist, to the holy Apostles Peter and Paul, and to all the saints, that I have sinned exceedingly in thought, word, and deed, *through my fault, through my fault, through my most grievous fault.*' I confessed on Saturday, three weeks ago, and received absolution, and I have performed the penance enjoined. Since then " — There she stopped.

There was a soft stir, as if she sank slowly down, and another as if she rose up again, and in a moment she said:

"Olive *is* my child. The picture I showed to Jean Thompson is the half-sister of my daughter's father, dead before my child was born. She is the image of her and of him; but, O God! Thou knowest! Oh, Olive, my own daughter!"

She ceased, and was still. Père Jerome waited, but no sound came. He looked through the window. She was kneeling, with her forehead resting on her arms — motionless.

He repeated the words of absolution. Still she did not stir.

"My daughter," he said, "go to thy home in peace." But she did not move.

He rose hastily, stepped from the box, raised her in his arms, and called her by name:

"Madame Delphine!" Her head fell back in his

elbow; for an instant there was life in the eyes — it glimmered — it vanished, and tears gushed from his own and fell upon the gentle face of the dead, as he looked up to heaven and cried:

"Lord, lay not this sin to her charge!"

Café des Exilés

CAFÉ DES EXILÉS.

THAT which in 1835 — I think he said thirty-five
— was a reality in the Rue Burgundy — I think he
said Burgundy — is now but a reminiscence. Yet so
vividly was its story told me, that at this moment the
old Café des Exilés appears before my eye, floating in
the clouds of revery, and I doubt not I see it just as
it was in the old times.

An antiquated story-and-a-half Creole cottage sitting right down on the banquette, as do the Choctaw
squaws who sell bay and sassafras and life-everlasting,
with a high, close board-fence shutting out of view
the diminutive garden on the southern side. An ancient willow droops over the roof of round tiles, and
partly hides the discolored stucco, which keeps dropping off into the garden as though the old café was
stripping for the plunge into oblivion — disrobing for
its execution. I see, well up in the angle of the broad
side gable, shaded by its rude awning of clapboards,
as the eyes of an old dame are shaded by her wrinkled
hand, the window of Pauline. Oh for the image of
the maiden, were it but for one moment, leaning out
of the casement to hang her mocking-bird and looking

down into the garden, — where, above the barrier of
old boards, I see the top of the fig-tree, the pale green
clump of bananas, the tall palmetto with its jagged
crown, Pauline's own two orange-trees holding up
their hands toward the window, heavy with the prom-
ises of autumn; the broad, crimson mass of the many-
stemmed oleander, and the crisp boughs of the pomegranate loaded with freckled apples, and with here
and there a lingering scarlet blossom.

The Café des Exilés, to use a figure, flowered, bore
fruit, and dropped it long ago — or rather Time and
Fate, like some uncursed Adam and Eve, came side
by side and cut away its clusters, as we sever the
golden burden of the banana from its stem; then,
like a banana which has borne its fruit, it was razed
to the ground and made way for a newer, brighter
growth. I believe it would set every tooth on edge
should I go by there now, — now that I have heard
the story, — and see the old site covered by the "Shoo-
fly Coffee-house." Pleasanter far to close my eyes
and call to view the unpretentious portals of the old
café, with her children — for such those exiles seem
to me — dragging their rocking-chairs out, and sitting
in their wonted group under the long, out-reaching
eaves which shaded the banquette of the Rue Burgundy.

It was in 1835 that the Café des Exilés was, as one
might say, in full blossom. Old M. D'Hemecourt,
father of Pauline and host of the café, himself a refugee from San Domingo, was the cause — at least the
human cause — of its opening. As its white-curtained,

glazed doors expanded, emitting a little puff of his own cigarette smoke, it was like the bursting of catalpa blossoms, and the exiles came like bees, pushing into the tiny room to sip its rich variety of tropical sirups, its lemonades, its orangeades, its orgeats, its barley-waters, and its outlandish wines, while they talked of dear home — that is to say, of Barbadoes, of Martinique, of San Domingo, and of Cuba.

There were Pedro and Benigno, and Fernandez and Francisco, and Benito. Benito was a tall, swarthy man, with immense gray moustachios, and hair as harsh as tropical grass and gray as ashes. When he could spare his cigarette from his lips, he would tell you in a cavernous voice, and with a wrinkled smile, that he was " a-t-thorty-seveng."

There was Martinez of San Domingo, yellow as a canary, always sitting with one leg curled under him, and holding the back of his head in his knitted fingers against the back of his rocking-chair. Father, mother, brother, sisters, all, had been massacred in the struggle of '21 and '22; he alone was left to tell the tale, and told it often, with that strange, infantile insensibility to the solemnity of his bereavement so peculiar to Latin people.

But, besides these, and many who need no mention, there were two in particular, around whom all the story of the Café des Exilés, of old M. D'Hemecourt and of Pauline, turns as on a double centre. First, Manuel Mazaro, whose small, restless eyes were as black and bright as those of a mouse, whose light talk became his dark girlish face, and whose redundant

locks curled so prettily and so wonderfully black under
the fine white brim of his jaunty Panama. He had
the hands of a woman, save that the nails were stained
with the smoke of cigarettes. He could play the
guitar delightfully, and wore his knife down behind
his coat-collar.

The second was "Major" Galahad Shaughnessy.
I imagine I can see him, in his white duck, brass-
buttoned roundabout, with his sabreless belt peeping
out beneath, all his boyishness in his sea-blue eyes,
leaning lightly against the door-post of the Café des
Exilés as a child leans against his mother, running his
fingers over a basketful of fragrant limes, and watching his chance to strike some solemn Creole under the
fifth rib with a good old Irish joke.

Old D'Hemecourt drew him close to his bosom.
The Spanish Creoles were, as the old man termed
it, both cold and hot, but never warm. Major Shaughnessy was warm, and it was no uncommon thing to
find those two apart from the others, talking in an
undertone, and playing at *confidantes* like two school-
girls. The kind old man was at this time drifting
close up to his sixtieth year. There was much he
could tell of San Domingo, whither he had been carried from Martinique in his childhood, whence he had
become a refugee to Cuba, and thence to New Orleans
in the flight of 1809.

It fell one day to Manuel Mazaro's lot to discover,
by sauntering within earshot, that to Galahad Shaughnessy only, of all the children of the Café des Exilés,
the good host spoke long and confidentially concern-

ing his daughter. The words, half heard and mag nified like objects seem in a fog, meaning Manuel Mazaro knew not what, but made portentous by his suspicious nature, were but the old man's recital of the grinding he had got between the millstones of his poverty and his pride, in trying so long to sustain, for little Pauline's sake, that attitude before society which earns respect from a surface-viewing world. It was while he was telling this that Manuel Mazaro drew near; the old man paused in an embarrassed way; the Major, sitting sidewise in his chair, lifted his cheek from its resting-place on his elbow; and Mazaro, after standing an awkward moment, turned away with such an inward feeling as one may guess would arise in a heart full of Cuban blood, not unmixed with Indian.

As he moved off, M. D'Hemecourt resumed: that in a last extremity he had opened, partly from dire want, partly for very love to homeless souls, the Café des Exilés. He had hoped that, as strong drink and high words were to be alike unknown to it, it might not prejudice sensible people; but it had. He had no doubt they said among themselves, "She is an excel lent and beautiful girl and deserving all respect;" and respect they accorded, but their *respects* they never came to pay.

"A café is a café," said the old gentleman. "It is nod possib' to ezcape him, aldough de Café des Exilés is differen from de rez."

"It's different from the Café des Réfugiés," suggested the Irishman.

"Differen' as possib'," replied M. D'Hemecourt
He looked about upon the walls. The shelves were
luscious with ranks of cooling sirups which he alone
knew how to make. The expression of his face
changed from sadness to a gentle pride, which spoke
without words, saying — and let our story pause a
moment to hear it say:

"If any poor exile, from any island where guavas
or mangoes or plantains grow, wants a draught which
will make him see his home among the cocoa-palms,
behold the Café des Exilés ready to take the poor child
up and give him the breast! And if gold or silver he
has them not, why Heaven and Santa Maria, and
Saint Christopher bless him! It makes no difference.
Here is a rocking-chair, here a cigarette, and here a
light from the host's own tinder. He will pay when he
can."

As this easily pardoned pride said, so it often occurred; and if the newly come exile said his father
was a Spaniard — Come!" old M. D'Hemecourt
would cry; "another glass; it is an innocent drink;
my mother was a Castilian." But, if the exile said
his mother was a Frenchwoman, the glasses would be
forthcoming all the same, for "My father," the old
man would say, "was a Frenchman of Martinique,
with blood as pure as that wine and a heart as sweet
as this honey; come, a glass of orgeat;' and he
would bring it himself in a quart tumbler.

Now, there are jealousies and jealousies. There
are people who rise up quickly and kill, and there are
others who turn their hot thoughts over silently in

their minds as a brooding bird turns her eggs in the nest. Thus did Manuel Mazaro, and took it ill that Galahad should see a vision in the temple while he and all the brethren tarried without. Pauline had been to the Café des Exilés in some degree what the image of the Virgin was to their churches at home; and 'for her father to whisper her name to one and not to another was, it seemed to Mazaro, as if the old man, were he a sacristan, should say to some single worshiper, "Here, you may have this madonna; I make it a present to you." Or, if such was not the handsome young Cuban's feeling, such, at least, was the disguise his jealousy put on. If Pauline was to be handed down from her niche, why, then, farewell Café des Exilés. She was its preserving influence, she made the place holy; she was the burning candles on the altar. Surely the reader will pardon the pen that lingers in the mention of her.

And yet I know not how to describe the forbearing, unspoken tenderness with which all these exiles regarded the maiden. In the balmy afternoons, as I have said, they gathered about their mother's knee, that is to say, upon the banquette outside the door. There, lolling back in their rocking-chairs, they would pass the evening hours with oft-repeated tales of home; and the moon would come out and glide among the clouds like a silver barge among islands wrapped in mist, and they loved the silently gliding orb with a sort of worship, because from her soaring height she looked down at the same moment upon them and upon their homes in the far Ar tilles. It was somewhat thus

that they looked upon Pauline as she seemed to them
held up half way to heaven, they knew not how.   Ah
those who have been pilgrims ; who have wandered
out beyond harbor and light ; whom fate hath led in
lonely paths strewn with thorns and briers not of their
own sowing ; who, homeless in a land of homes, see
windows gleaming and doors ajar, but not for them, —
it is they who well understand what the worship is that
cries to any daughter of our dear mother Eve whose
footsteps chance may draw across the path, the silent,
beseeching cry, "Stay a little instant that I may look
upon you.   Oh, woman, beautifier of the earth!   Stay
till I recall the face of my sister ; stay yet a moment
while I look from afar, with helpless-hanging hands,
upon the softness of thy cheek, upon the folded coils
of thy shining hair ; and my spirit shall fall down and
say those prayers which I may never again — God
knoweth — say at home."

She was seldom seen ; but sometimes, when the
lounging exiles would be sitting in their afternoon
circle under the eaves, and some old man would tell
his tale of fire and blood and capture and escape, and
the heads would lean forward from the chair-backs
and a great stillness would follow the ending of the
story, old M. D'Hemecourt would all at once speak up
and say, laying his hands upon the narrator's knee,
"Comrade, your throat is dry, here are fresh limes ;
let my dear child herself come and mix you a lemonade."   Then the neighbors over the way, sitting about
their doors, would by and by softly say, "See, see!
there is Pauline!" and all the exiles would rise from

their rocking-chairs, take off their hats and stand as men stand in church, while Pauline came out like the moon from a cloud, descended the three steps of the café door, and stood with waiter and glass, a new Rebecca with her pitcher, before the swarthy wanderer.

What tales that would have been tear-compelling, nay, heart-rending, had they not been palpable inventions, the pretty, womanish Mazaro from time to time poured forth, in the ever ungratified hope that the goddess might come down with a draught of nectar for him, it profiteth not to recount ; but I should fail to show a family feature of the Café des Exilés did I omit to say that these make-believe adventures were heard with every mark of respect and credence ; while, on the other hand, they were never attempted in the presence of the Irishman. He would have moved an eyebrow, or made some barely audible sound, or dropped some seemingly innocent word, and the whole company, spite of themselves, would have smiled. Wherefore, it may be doubted whether at any time the curly-haired young Cuban had that playful affection for his Celtic comrade, which a habit of giving little velvet taps to Galahad's cheek made a show of.

Such was the Café des Exilés, such its inmates, such its guests, when certain apparently trivial events began to fall around it as germs of blight fall upon corn, and to bring about that end which cometh to all things.

The little seed of jealousy, dropped into the heart of Manuel Mazaro, we have already taken into account.

Galahad Shaughnessy began to be specially active in organizing a society of Spanish Americans, the de-

sign of which, as set forth in its manuscript constitu-
tion, was to provide proper funeral honors to such of
their membership as might be overtaken by death;
and, whenever it was practicable, to send their ashes
to their native land. Next to Galahad in this movement was an elegant old Mexican physician, Dr. ——,
— his name escapes me — whom the Café des Exilés
sometimes took upon her lap — that is to say door-step
— but whose favorite resort was the old Café des
Réfugiés in the Rue Royale (Royal Street, as it was
beginning to be called). Manuel Mazaro was made
secretary.

It was for some reason thought judicious for the
society to hold its meetings in various places, now
here, now there; but the most frequent rendezvous
was the Café des Exilés; it was quiet; those Spanish
Creoles, however they may afterward cackle, like to
lay their plans noiselessly, like a hen in a barn.
There was a very general confidence in this old institution, a kind of inward assurance that "mother
wouldn't tell;" though, after all, what great secrets
could there be connected with a mere burial society?

Before the hour of meeting, the Café des Exilés
always sent away her children and closed her door.
Presently they would commence returning, one by one,
as a flock of wild fowl will do, that has been startled
up from its accustomed haunt. Frequenters of the
Café des Réfugiés also would appear. A small gate
in the close garden-fence let them into a room behind
the café proper, and by and by the apartment would
be full of dark-visaged men conversing in the low,

courteous tone common to their race. The shutters of doors and windows were closed and the chinks stopped with cotton; some people are so jealous of observation.

On a certain night after one of these meetings had dispersed in its peculiar way, the members retiring two by two at intervals, Manuel Mazaro and M. D'Hemecourt were left alone, sitting close together in the dimly lighted room, the former speaking, the other, with no pleasant countenance, attending. It seemed to the young Cuban a proper precaution — he was made of precautions — to speak in English. His voice was barely audible.

"—— sayce to me, 'Manuel, she t-theeng I want-n to marry hore.' Señor, you shouth 'ave see' him laugh!"

M. D'Hemecourt lifted up his head, and laid his hand upon the young man's arm.

"Manuel Mazaro," he began, "iv dad w'ad you say is nod" —

The Cuban interrupted.

"If is no' t-thrue you will keel Manuel Mazaro? — a' r-r-right-a!"

"No," said the tender old man, "no, bud h-I am positeef dad de Madjor will shood you."

Mazaro nodded, and lifted one finger for attention.

"—— sayce to me, 'Manuel, you goin' tell-a Señor D'Hemecourt, I fin'-a you some nigh' an' cut-a you' heart ou'. An' I sayce to heem-a, 'Boat-a if Señor D'Hemecourt he fin'-in' ou' frone Pauline'"—

"*Silence!*" fiercely cried the old man. "My God!

'Sieur Mazaro, neider you, neider somebody helse s'all h'use de nem of me daughter. It is nod possib' dad you s'all spick him! I cannot pearmid thad."

While the old man was speaking these vehement words, the Cuban was emphatically nodding approval.

"Co-rect-a, co-rect-a, Señor," he replied. "Señor, you' r-r-right-a; escuse-a me, Señor, escuse-a me. Señor D'Hemecourt, Mayor Shaughness', when he talkin' wi' me he usin' hore-a name o the t-thime-a!"

"My fren'," said M. D'Hemecourt, rising and speaking with labored control, "I muz tell you good nighd. You 'ave sooprise me a verry gred deal. I s'all *in*vestigade doze ting; an', Manuel Mazaro, h-I am a hole man; bud I will requez you, iv dad wad you say is nod de true, my God! not to h-ever ritturn again ad de Café des Exilés."

Mazaro smiled and nodded. His host opened the door into the garden, and, as the young man stepped out, noticed even then how handsome was his face and figure, and how the odor of the night jasmine was filling the air with an almost insupportable sweetness. The Cuban paused a moment, as if to speak, but checked himself, lifted his girlish face, and looked up to where the daggers of the palmetto-tree were crossed upon the face of the moon, dropped his glance, touched his Panama, and silently followed by the bare-headed old man, drew open the little garden-gate, looked cautiously out, said good-night, and stepped into the street.

As M. D'Hemecourt returned to the door through which he had come, he uttered an ejaculation of aston blment. Pauline stood before him. She spoke hurriedly in French.

"Papa, papa, it is not true."

"No, my child," he responded, "I am sure it is not true; I am sure it is all false; but why do I find you out of bed so late, little bird? The night is nearly gone."

He laid his hand upon her cheek.

"Ah, papa, I cannot deceive you. I thought Manuel would tell you something of this kind, and I listened."

The father's face immediately betrayed a new and deeper distress.

"Pauline, my child," he said with tremulous voice, "if Manuel's story is all false, in the name of Heaven how could you think he was going to tell it?"

He unconsciously clasped his hands. The good child had one trait which she could not have inherited from her father; she was quick-witted and discerning; yet now she stood confounded.

"Speak, my child," cried the alarmed old man; "speak! let me live, and not die."

"Oh, papa," she cried, "I do not know!"

The old man groaned.

"Papa, papa," she cried again, "I felt it; I know not how; something told me."

"Alas!" exclaimed the old man, "if it was your conscience!"

"No, no, no, papa," cried Pauline, "but I was afraid of Manuel Mazaro, and I think he hates him —and I think he will hurt him in any way he can

—and I *know* he will even try to kill him. Oh! my God!"

She struck her hands together above her head, and burst into a flood of tears. Her father looked upon her with such sad sternness as his tender nature was capable of. He laid hold of one of her arms to draw a hand from the face whither both hands had gone.

"You know something else," he said; "you know that the Major loves you, or you think so: is it not true?"

She dropped both hands, and, lifting her streaming eyes that had nothing to hide straight to his, suddenly said:

"I would give worlds to think so!" and sunk upon the floor.

He was melted and convinced in one instant.

"Oh, my child, my child," he cried, trying to lift her. "Oh, my poor little Pauline, your papa is not angry. Rise, my little one; so; kiss me; Heaven bless thee. Pauline, treasure, what shall I do with thee? Where shall I hide thee?"

"You have my counsel already, papa."

"Yes, my child, and you were right. The Café des Exilés never should have been opened. It is no place for you; no place at all."

"Let us leave it," said Pauline.

"Ah! Pauline, I would close it to-morrow if I could, but now it is too late; I cannot."

"Why?" asked Pauline, pleadingly.

She had cast an arm about his neck. Her tears sparkled with a smile.

" My daughter, I cannot tell you; you must go now to bed; good-night — or good-morning; God keep you! "

" Well, then, papa," she said, " have no fear; you need not hide me; I have my prayer-book, and my altar, and my garden, and my window; my garden is my fenced city, and my window my watch-tower; do you see?"

" Ah! Pauline," responded the father, " but I have been letting the enemy in and out at pleasure."

" Good-night," she answered, and kissed him three times on either cheek; " the blessed Virgin will take care of us; good-night; *he* never said those things; not he; good-night."

The next evening Galahad Shaughnessy and Manuel Mazaro met at that " very different" place, the Café des Réfugiés. There was much free talk going on about Texan annexation, about chances of war with Mexico, about San Domingan affairs, about Cuba and many et-ceteras. Galahad was in his usual gay mood. He strode about among a mixed company of Louisianais, Cubans, and Américains, keeping them in a great laugh with his account of one of Ole Bull's concerts, and how he had there extorted an invitation from M. and Mme. Devoti to attend one of their famous children's fancy dress balls.

" Halloo! " said he as Mazaro approached, " heer's the etheerial Angelica herself. Look-ut heer, sissy, why ar'n't ye in the maternal arms of the Café des Exilés?"

Mazaro smiled amiably and sat down. A moment

after, the Irishman, stepping away from his com panions, stood before the young Cuban, and asked, with a quiet business air:

"D'ye want to see me, Mazaro?"

The Cuban nodded, and they went aside. Mazaro, in a few quick words, looking at his pretty foot the while, told the other on no account to go near the Café des Exilés, as there were two men hanging about there, evidently watching for him, and—

"Wut's the use o' that?" asked Galahad; "I say, wut's the use o' that?"

Major Shaughnessy's habit of repeating part of his words arose from another, of interrupting any person who might be speaking.

"They must know—I say they must know that whenever I'm nowhurs else I'm heer. What do they want?"

Mazaro made a gesture, signifying caution and secrecy, and smiled, as if to say, "You ought to know."

"Aha!" said the Irishman softly. "Why don't they come here?"

"Z-afrai'," said Mazaro; "d'they frai' to do an'teen een d-these-a crowth."

"That's so," said the Irishman; "I say, that's so. If I don't feel very much like go-un, I'll not go; I say, I'll not go. We've no business to-night, eh, Mazaro?"

"No, Señor."

A second evening was much the same, Mazaro re- peating his warning. But when, on the third evening, the Irishman again repeated his willingness to stay away from the Café des Exilés unless he should feel strongly impelled to go, it was with the mental reservation that he did feel very much in that humor, and, unknown to Mazaro, should thither repair, if only to see whether some of those deep old fellows were not contriving a practical joke.

"Mazaro," said he, "I'm go-un around the caurnur a bit; I want ye to wait heer till I come back. I say I want ye to wait heer till I come back; I'll be gone about three-quarters of an hour."

Mazaro assented. He saw with satisfaction the Irishman start in a direction opposite that in which lay the Café des Exilés, tarried fifteen or twenty minutes, and then, thinking he could step around to the Café des Exilés and return before the expiration of the allotted time, hurried out.

Meanwhile that peaceful habitation sat in the moonlight with her children about her feet. The company outside the door was somewhat thinner than common. M. D'Hemecourt was not among them, but was sitting in the room behind the café. The long table which the burial society used at their meetings extended across the apartment, and a lamp had been placed upon it. M. D'Hemecourt sat by the lamp. Opposite him was a chair, which seemed awaiting an expected occupant. Beside the old man sat Pauline. They were talking in cautious undertones, and in French.

No," she seemed to insist; "we do not know that he refuses to come. We only know that Manuel says so."

The father shook his head sadly. "When has he ever staid away three nights together before?" he asked. "No, my child; it is intentional. Manuel urges him to come, but he only sends poor excuses."

"But," said the girl, shading her face from the lamp and speaking with some suddenness, "why have you not sent word to him by some other person?"

M. D'Hemecourt looked up at his daughter a moment, and then smiled at his own simplicity.

"Ah!" he said. "Certainly; and that is what I will — run away, Pauline. There is Manuel, now, ahead of time!"

A step was heard inside the café. The maiden, though she knew the step was not Mazaro's, rose hastily, opened the nearest door, and disappeared. She had barely closed it behind her when Galahad Shaughnessy entered the apartment.

M'Hemecourt rose up, both surprised and confused.

"Good-evening, Munsher D'Himecourt," said the Irishman. "Munsher D'Himecourt, I know it's against rules — I say, I know it's against rules to come in here, but " — smiling, — "I want to have a private wurd with ye. I say, I want to have a private wurd with ye."

In the closet of bottles the maiden smiled triumphantly. She also wiped the dew from her forehead, for the place was very close and warm.

With her father was no triumph. In him sadness and doubt were so mingled with anger that he dared not lift his eyes, but gazed at the knot in the wood of the table, which looked like a caterpillar curled up

Mazaro, he concluded, had really asked the Major to come.

"Mazaro tol' you?" he asked.

"Yes," answered the Irishman. "Mazaro told me I was watched, and asked" —

"Madjor," unluckily interrupted the old man, suddenly looking up and speaking with subdued fervor, "for w'y — iv Mazaro tol' you — for w'y you din come more sooner? Dad is one 'eavy charge again' you."

"Didn't Mazaro tell ye why I didn't come?" asked the other, beginning to be puzzled at his host's meaning.

"Yez," replied M. D'Hemecourt, "bud one brev zhenteman should not be afraid of" —

The young man stopped him with a quiet laugh. "Munsher D'Himecourt," said he, "I'm nor afraid of any two men living — I say I'm nor afraid of any two men living, and certainly not of the two that's bean a-watchin' me lately, if they're the two I think they are."

M. D'Hemecourt flushed in a way quite incomprehensible to the speaker, who nevertheless continued:

"It was the charges," he said, with some slyness in his smile. "They *are* heavy, as ye say, and that's the very reason — I say that's the very reason why I staid away, ye see, eh? I say that's the very reason I staid away."

Then, indeed, there was a dew for the maiden to wipe from her brow, unconscious that every word that was being said bore a different significance in the mind of each of the three. The old man was agitated.

"Bud, sir," he began, shaking his head and lifting his hand.

"Bless yer soul, Munsher D'Himecourt," interrupted the Irishman. "Wut's the use o' grapplin' two cut-throats, when "—

"Madjor Shaughnessy!" cried M. D'Hemecourt, losing all self-control. "H-I am nod a cud-troad, Madjor Shaughnessy, h-an I 'ave a r-r-righd to wadge you."

The Major rose from his chair.

"What d'ye mean?" he asked vacantly, and then: "Look-ut here, Munsher D'Himecourt, one of uz is crazy. I say one "—

"No, sar-r-r!" cried the other, rising and clenching his trembling fist. "H-I am not crezzy. I 'ave de righd to wadge dad man wad mague rimark aboud me dotter."

"I never did no such a thing."

"You did."

"I never did no such a thing."

"Bud you 'ave jus hacknowledge'—"

"I never did no such a *thing,* I tell ye, and the man that's told ye so is a liur!"

"Ah-h-h-h!" said the old man, wagging his finger. "Ah-h-h-h! You call Manuel Mazaro one liar?"

The Irishman laughed out.

"Well, I should say so!"

He motioned the old man into his chair, and both sat down again.

"Why, Munsher D'Himecourt, Mazaro's been keepin' me away from heer with a yarn about two

Spaniards watchin' for me. That's what I came in to ask ye about. My dear sur, do ye s'pose I wud talk about the goddess — I mean, yer daughter — to the likes o' Mazaro — I say to the likes o' Mazaro?''

To say the old man was at sea would be too feeble an expression — he was in the trough of the sea, with a hurricane of doubts and fears whirling around him. Somebody had told a lie, and he, having struck upon its sunken surface, was dazed and stunned. He opened his lips to say he knew not what, when his ear caught the voice of Manuel Mazaro, replying to the greeting of some of his comrades outside the front door.

"He is comin'!" cried the old man. "Mague you'sev hide, Madjor; do not led 'im kedge you, Mon Dieu!"

The Irishman smiled.

"The little yellow wretch!" said he quietly, his blue eyes dancing. "I'm goin' to catch *him*.''

A certain hidden hearer instantly made up her mind to rush out between the two young men and be a heroine.

"*Non, non!*" exclaimed M. D'Hemecourt excitedly. "Nod in de Café des Exilés — nod now, Madjor. Go in dad door, hif you pliz, Madjor. You will heer 'im w'at he 'ave to say. Mague you'sev de troub'. Nod dad door — diz one.''

The Major laughed again and started toward the door indicated, but in an instant stopped.

"I can't go in theyre,'' he said. "That's yer daughter's room.''

"*Oui, oui, mais!*" cried the other softly, but Mazaro's step was near.

"I'll just slip in heer," and the amused Shaughnessy tripped lightly to the closet door, drew it open in spite of a momentary resistance from within which he had no time to notice, stepped into a small recess full of shelves and bottles, shut the door, and stood face to face — the broad moonlight shining upon her through a small, high-grated opening on one side — with Pauline. At the same instant the voice of the young Cuban sounded in the room.

Pauline was in a great tremor. She made as if she would have opened the door and fled, but the Irishman gave a gesture of earnest protest and re-assurance. The re-opened door might make the back parlor of the Café des Exilés a scene of blood. Thinking of this, what could she do? She staid.

"You goth a heap-a thro-vle, Señor," said Manuel Mazaro, taking the seat so lately vacated. He had patted M. D'Hemecourt tenderly on the back and the old gentleman had flinched; hence the remark, to which there was no reply.

"Was a bee crowth a' the *Café the Réfugiés,*" continued the young man.

"Bud, w'ere dad Madjor Shaughnessy?" demanded M. D'Hemecourt, with the little sternness he could command.

"Mayor Shaughness'—yez-a; was there; boat-a," with a disparaging smile and shake of the head, "he woon-a come-a to you, Señor, oh! no.'

The old man smiled bitterly.

" *Non?* " he asked.

" Oh, no, Señor ! " Mazaro drew his chair closer. " Señor ; " he paused, — " eez a-vary bath-a fore-a you thaughter, eh? "

" W'at? " asked the host, snapping like a tormented dog.

" D-theze talkin' 'bou', " answered the young man ; d-theze coffee-howces noth a goo' plaze-a fore hore, eh? "

The Irishman and the maiden looked into each other's eyes an instant, as people will do when listening ; but Pauline's immediately fell, and when Mazaro's words were understood, her blushes became visible even by moonlight.

" He's r-right ! " emphatically whispered Galahad.

She attempted to draw back a step, but found herself against the shelves. M. D'Hemecourt had not answered. Mazaro spoke again.

" Boat-a you canno' help-a, eh? I know, 'out-a she gettin' marry, eh? "

Pauline trembled. Her father summoned all his force and rose as if to ask his questioner to leave him ; but the handsome Cuban motioned him down with a gesture that seemed to beg for only a moment more.

" Señor, if a-was one man whath lo-va you' thaughter, all is possiblee to lo-va. "

Pauline, nervously braiding some bits of wire which she had unconsciously taken from a shelf, glanced up — against her will, — into the eyes of Galahad. They were looking so steadily down upon her that with a great leap of the heart for joy she closed her own and half turned away. But Mazaro had not ceased.

"All is possiblee to lo-va, Señor, you shouth-a let marry hore an' tak'n 'way frone d'these plaze, Señor."

"Manuel Mazaro," said M. D'Hemecourt, again rising, "you 'ave say enough."

"No, no, Señor; no, no; I want tell-a you — *is* a-one man — *whath lo-va* you' thaughter; an' I *knowce* him!"

Was there no cause for quarrel, after all? Could it be that Mazaro was about to speak for Galahad? The old man asked in his simplicity:

"Madjor Shaughnessy?"

Mazaro smiled mockingly.

"Mayor Shaughness'," he said; "oh, no; not Mayor Shaughness'!"

Pauline could stay no longer; escape she must, though it be in Manuel Mazaro's very face. Turning again and looking up into Galahad's face in a great fright, she opened her lips to speak, but —

"Mayor Shaughness'," continued the Cuban; "*he* nev'r-a lo-va you' thaughter."

Galahad was putting the maiden back from the door with his hand.

"Pauline," he said, "it's a lie!"

"An', Señor," pursued the Cuban, "if a was possiblee you' thaughter to lo-va heem, a-wouth-a be worse-a kine in worlt; but, Señor, *I*" —

M. D'Hemecourt made a majestic sign for silence. He had resumed his chair, but he rose up once more, took the Cuban's hat from the table and tendered it to him.

"Manuel Mazaro, you 'ave "—

"Señor, I goin' tell you "—

"Manuel Mazaro, you "—

"Boat-a Señor "—

"Bud, Manuel Maz " —

"Señor, escuse-a me "—

"Huzh !" cried the old man. "Manuel Mazaro, **you** ave deceive' me ! You 'ave *mocque* me, Manu "—

"Señor," cried Mazaro, "I swear-a to you that all-a what I sayin' ees-a "—

He stopped aghast. Galahad and Pauline stood before him.

"Is what ?" asked the blue-eyed man, with a look of quiet delight on his face, such as Mazaro instantly remembered to have seen on it one night when Galahad was being shot at in the Sucking Calf Restaurant in St. Peter Street.

The table was between them, but Mazaro's hand went upward toward the back of his coat-collar.

"Ah, ah !" cried the Irishman, shaking his head with a broader smile and thrusting his hand threateningly into his breast ; "don't ye do that ! just finish yer speech."

"Was-a notthin'," said the Cuban, trying to smile back.

"Yer a liur," said Galahad.

"No," said Mazaro, still endeavoring to smile through his agony ; "z-was on'y tellin' Señor D'Hemecourt someteen z-was t-thrue."

"And I tell ye," said Galahad, "ye'r a liur, and to be so kind an' get yersel' to the front stoop, as I'm desiruz o' kickin' ye before the crowd."

"Madjor!" cried D'Hemecourt —

"Go," said Galahad, advancing a step toward the Cuban.

Had Manuel Mazaro wished to personate the prince of darkness, his beautiful face had the correct expression for it. He slowly turned, opened the door into the café, sent one glowering look behind, and disappeared.

Pauline laid her hand upon her lover's arm.

"Madjor," began her father.

"Oh, Madjor and Madjor," said the Irishman; "Munsher D'Hemecourt, just say 'Madjor, heer's a gude wife fur ye,' and I'll let the little serpent go."

Thereupon, sure enough, both M. D'Hemecourt and his daughter, rushing together, did what I have been hoping all along, for the reader's sake, they would have dispensed with; they burst into tears; whereupon the Major, with his Irish appreciation of the ludicrous, turned away to hide his smirk and began good-humoredly to scratch himself first on the temple and then on the thigh.

Mazaro passed silently through the group about the door-steps, and not many minutes afterward, Galahad Shaughnessy, having taken a place among the exiles, rose with the remark that the old gentleman would doubtless be willing to tell them good-night. Good-night was accordingly said, the Café des Exilés closed her windows, then her doors, winked a moment or two through the cracks in the shutters and then went fast asleep.

The Mexican physician, at Galahad's request, told Mazaro that at the next meeting of the burial society he might and must occupy his accustomed seat without fear of molestation.; and he did so.

The meeting took place some seven days after the affair in the back parlor, and on the same ground. Business being finished, Galahad, who presided, stood up, looking, in his white duck suit among his darkly-clad companions, like a white sheep among black ones, and begged leave to order "dlasses" from the front room. I say among black sheep; yet, I suppose, than that double row of languid, effeminate faces, one would have been taxed to find a more harmless-looking company. The glasses were brought and filled.

"Gentlemen," said Galahad, "comrades, this may be the last time we ever meet together an unbroken body."

Martinez of San Domingo, he of the horrible experience, nodded with a lurking smile, curled a leg under him and clasped his fingers behind his head.

"Who knows," continued the speaker, "but Señor Benito, though strong and sound and har'ly thirty-seven"—here all smiled—"may be taken ill to-morrow?"

Martinez smiled across to the tall, gray Benito on Galahad's left, and he, in turn, smilingly showed to the company a thin, white line of teeth between his moustachios like distant reefs.

"Who knows," the young Irishman proceeded to inquire, "I say, who knows but Pedro, theyre, may be struck wid a fever?"

Pedro, a short, compact man of thoroughly mixed

blood, and with an eyebrow cut away, whose surname
no one knew, smiled his acknowledgments.

"Who knows?" resumed Galahad, when those who
understood English had explained in Spanish to those
who did not, "but they may soon need the services
not only of our good doctor heer, but of our society;
and that Fernandez and Benigno, and Gonzalez and
Dominguez, may not be chosen to see, on that very
schooner lying at the Picayune Tier just now, their
beloved remains and so forth safely delivered into the
hands and lands of their people. I say, who knows
bur it may be so!"

The company bowed graciously as who should say,
"Well-turned phrases, Señor — well-turned."

"And *amigos*, if so be that such is their approoching
fate, I will say:"

He lifted his glass, and the rest did the same.

"I say, I will say to them, Creoles, countrymen,
and lovers, boun voyadge an' good luck to ye's."

For several moments there was much translating,
bowing, and murmured acknowledgments; Mazaro
said: "*Bueno!*" and all around among the long
double rank of moustachioed lips amiable teeth were
gleaming, some white, some brown, some yellow, like
bones in the grass.

"And now, gentlemen," Galahad recommenced,
"fellow-exiles, once more. Munsher D'Himecourt, it
was yer practice, until lately, to reward a good talker
with a dlass from the hands o' yer daughter." (*Si,
si!*) "I'm bur a poor speaker." (*Si, si, Señor, z-a-
fine-a kin'-a can be; si!*) "However, I'll ask ye,

not knowun bur it may be the last time we all meet together, if ye will not let the goddess of the Café des Exilés grace our company with her presence for just about one minute?" (*Yez-a, Señor; si; yez-a; oui.*)

Every head was turned toward the old man, nodding the echoed request.

"Ye see, friends," said Galahad in a true Irish whisper, as M. D'Hemecourt left the apartment, " her poseetion has been a-growin' more and more embarrassin' daily, and the operaytions of our society were likely to make it wurse in the future ; wherefore I have lately taken steps — I say I tuke steps this morn to relieve the old gentleman's distresses and his daughter's " —

He paused. M. D'Hemecourt entered with Pauline, and the exiles all rose up. Ah ! — but why say again she was lovely?

Galahad stepped forward to meet her, took her hand, led her to the head of the board, and turning to the company, said :

"Friends and fellow-patriots, Misthress Shaughnessy."

There was no outburst of astonishment — only the same old bowing, smiling, and murmuring of compliment. Galahad turned with a puzzled look to M. D'Hemecourt, and guessed the truth. In the joy of an old man's heart he had already that afternoon told the truth to each and every man separately, as a secret too deep for them to reveal, but too sweet for him to keep. The Major and Pauline were man and wife.

The last laugh that was ever heard in the Café des Exilés sounded softly through the room.

"Lads," said the Irishman. "Fill yer glasses. Here's to the Café des Exilés, God bless her!"

And the meeting slowly adjourned.

Two days later, signs and rumors of sickness began to find place about the Café des Réfugiés, and the Mexican physician made three calls in one day. It was said by the people around that the tall Cuban gentleman named Benito was very sick in one of the back rooms. A similar frequency of the same physician's calls was noticed about the Café des Exilés.

"The man with one eyebrow," said the neighbors, "is sick. Pauline left the house yesterday to make room for him."

"Ah! is it possible?"

"Yes, it is really true; she and her husband. She took her mocking-bird with her; he carried it; he came back alone."

On the next afternoon the children about the Café des Réfugiés enjoyed the spectacle of the invalid Cuban moved on a trestle to the Café des Exilés, although he did not look so deathly sick as they could have liked to see him, and on the fourth morning the doors of the Café des Exilés remained closed. A black-bordered funeral notice, veiled with crape, announced that the great Caller-home of exiles had served his summons upon Don Pedro Hernandez (surname borrowed for the occasion), and Don Carlos Mendez y Benito.

The hour for the funeral was fixed at four P.M. It

never took place. Down at the Picayune Tier on the river bank there was, about two o'clock that same day, a slight commotion, and those who stood aimlessly about a small, neat schooner, said she was "seized." At four there suddenly appeared before the Café des Exilés a squad of men with silver crescents on their breasts—police officers. The old cottage sat silent with closed doors, the crape hanging heavily over the funeral notice like a widow's veil, the little unseen garden sending up odors from its hidden censers, and the old weeping-willow bending over all.

"Nobody here?" asks the leader.

The crowd which has gathered stares without answering.

As quietly and peaceably as possible the officers pry open the door. They enter, and the crowd pushes in after. There are the two coffins, looking very heavy and solid, lying in state but unguarded.

The crowd draws a breath of astonishment. "Are they going to wrench the tops off with hatchet and chisel?"

Rap, rap, rap; wrench, rap, wrench. Ah! the cases come open.

"Well kept?" asks the leader flippantly.

"Oh, yes," is the reply. And then all laugh.

One of the lookers-on pushes up and gets a glimpse within.

"What is it?" ask the other idlers.

He tells one quietly.

"What did he say?" ask the rest, one of another.

"He says they are not dead men, but new muskets" —

"Here, clear out!" cries an officer, and the loiterers fall back and by and by straggle off.

The exiles? What became of them, do you ask? Why, nothing; they were not troubled, but they never all came together again. Said a chief-of-police to Major Shaughnessy years afterward:

"Major, there was only one thing that kept your expedition from succeeding — you were too sly about it. Had you come out flat and said what you were doing, we'd never a-said a word to you. But that little fellow gave us the wink, and then we had to stop you."

And was no one punished? Alas! one was. Poor, pretty, curly-headed traitorous Mazaro! He was drawn out of Carondelet Canal — cold, dead! And when his wounds were counted — they were just the number of the Café des Exilés' children, less Galahad. But the mother — that is, the old café — did not see it; she had gone up the night before in a chariot of fire.

In the files of the old "Picayune" and "Price-Current" of 1837 may be seen the mention of Galahad Shaughnessy among the merchants — "our enterprising and accomplished fellow-townsman," and all that. But old M. D'Hemecourt's name is cut in marble, and his citizenship is in "a city whose maker and builder is God."

Only yesterday I dined with the Shaughnessys — fine old couple and handsome. Their children sat about them and entertained me most pleasantly. But

there isn't one can tell a tale as their father can —
'twas he told me this one, though here and there my
enthusiasm may have taken liberties. He knows the
history of every old house in the French Quarter; or,
if he happens not to know a true one, he can make one
up as he goes along.

Belles Demoiselles Plantation

BELLES DEMOISELLES PLANTATION.

THE original grantee was Count ——, assume the name to be De Charleu; the old Creoles never forgive a public mention. He was the French king's commissary. One day, called to France to explain the lucky accident of the commissariat having burned down with his account-books inside, he left his wife, a Choctaw Comptesse, behind.

Arrived at court, his excuses were accepted, and that tract granted him where afterwards stood Belles Demoiselles Plantation. A man cannot remember every thing! In a fit of forgetfulness he married a French gentlewoman, rich and beautiful, and "brought her out." However, "All's well that ends well;" a famine had been in the colony, and the Choctaw Comptesse had starved, leaving nought but a half-caste orphan family lurking on the edge of the settlement, bearing our French gentlewoman's own new name, and being mentioned in Monsieur's will.

And the new Comptesse—she tarried but a twelve-month, left Monsieur a lovely son, and departed, led out of this vain world by the swamp-fever.

From this son sprang the proud Creole family of

De Charleu. It rose straight up, up, up, generation after generation, tall, branchless, slender, palm-like; and finally, in the time of which I am to tell, flowered with all the rare beauty of a century-plant, in Artemise, Innocente, Felicité, the twins Marie and Martha, Leontine and little Septima; the seven beautiful daughters for whom their home had been fitly named Belles Demoiselles.

The Count's grant had once been a long Pointe, round which the Mississippi used to whirl, and seethe, and foam, that it was horrid to behold. Big whirlpools would open and wheel about in the savage eddies under the low bank, and close up again, and others open, and spin, and disappear. Great circles of muddy surface would boil up from hundreds of feet below, and gloss over, and seem to float away, — sink, come back again under water, and with only a soft hiss surge up again, and again drift off, and vanish. Every few minutes the loamy bank would tip down a great load of earth upon its besieger, and fall back a foot, — sometimes a yard, — and the writhing river would press after, until at last the Pointe was quite swallowed up, and the great river glided by in a majestic curve, and asked no more; the bank stood fast, the "caving" became a forgotten misfortune, and the diminished grant was a long, sweeping, willowy bend, rustling with miles of sugar-cane.

Coming up the Mississippi in the sailing craft of those early days, about the time one first could descry the white spires of the old St. Louis Cathedral, you would be pretty sure to spy, just over to your right under the levee, Belles Demoiselles Mansion, with its broad veranda and red painted cypress roof, peering over the embankment, like a bird in the nest, half hid by the avenue of willows which one of the departed De Charleus,—he that married a Marot,—had planted on the levee's crown.

The house stood unusually near the river, facing eastward, and standing four-square, with an immense veranda about its sides, and a flight of steps in front spreading broadly downward, as we open arms to a child. From the veranda nine miles of river were seen ; and in their compass, near at hand, the shady garden full of rare and beautiful flowers ; farther away broad fields of cane and rice, and the distant quarters of the slaves, and on the horizon everywhere a dark belt of cypress forest.

The master was old Colonel De Charleu,—Jean Albert Henri Joseph De Charleu-Marot, and "Colonel" by the grace of the first American governor. Monsieur,—he would not speak to any one who called him "Colonel," — was a hoary-headed patriarch. His step was firm, his form erect, his intellect strong and clear, his countenance classic, serene, dignified, commanding, his manners courtly, his voice musical, —fascinating. He had had his vices,—all his life ; but had borne them, as his race do, with a serenity of conscience and a cleanness of mouth that left no outward blemish on the surface of the gentleman. He had gambled in Royal Street, drunk hard in Orleans Street, run his adversary through in the duelling-ground at Slaughter-house Point, and danced and

quarrelled at the St. Philippe-street-theatre quadroon
balls. Even now, with all his courtesy and bounty,
and a hospitality which seemed to be entertaining
angels, he was bitter-proud and penurious, and deep
down in his hard-finished heart loved nothing but him
self, his name, and his motherless children. But
these! — their ravishing beauty was all but excuse
enough for the unbounded idolatry of their father.
Against these seven goddesses he never rebelled.
Had they even required him to defraud old De
Carlos —

I can hardly say.

Old De Carlos was his extremely distant relative on
the Choctaw side. With this single exception, the
narrow thread-like line of descent from the Indian
wife, diminished to a mere strand by injudicious alli-
ances, and deaths in the gutters of old New Orleans,
was extinct. The name, by Spanish contact, had
become De Carlos; but this one surviving bearer of it
was known to all, and known only, as Injin Charlie.

One thing I never knew a Creole to do. He will
not utterly go back on the ties of blood, no matter
what sort of knots those ties may be. For one reason, he is never ashamed of his or his father's sins;
and for another, — he will tell you — he is " all
heart!' "

So the different heirs of the De Charleu estate had
always strictly regarded the rights and interests of the
De Carloses, especially their ownership of a block of
dilapidated buildings in a part of the city, which had
once been very poor property, but was beginning to be

valuable. This block had much more than maintained
the last De Carlos through a long and lazy lifetime,
and, as his household consisted only of himself, and
an aged and crippled negress, the inference was irre-
sistible that he "had money." Old Charlie, though
by *alias* an "Injin," was plainly a dark white man,
about as old as Colonel De Charleu, sunk in the bliss
of deep ignorance, shrewd, deaf, and, by repute at
least, unmerciful.

The Colonel and he always conversed in English.
This rare accomplishment, which the former had
learned from his Scotch wife, — the latter from up-
river traders, — they found an admirable medium of
communication, answering, better than French could, a
similar purpose to that of the stick which we fasten to
the bit of one horse and breast-gear of another, whereby each keeps his distance. Once in a while, too, by
way of jest, English found its way among the ladies
of Belles Demoiselles, always signifying that their
sire was about to have business with old Charlie.

Now a long-standing wish to buy out Charlie troubled
the Colonel. He had no desire to oust him unfairly ;
he was proud of being always fair ; yet he did long to
engross the whole estate under one title. Out of his
luxurious idleness he had conceived this desire, and
thought little of so slight an obstacle as being already
somewhat in debt to old Charlie for money borrowed,
and for which Belles Demoiselles was, of course, good,
ten times over. Lots, buildings, rents, all, might as well
be his. he thought, to give, keep, or destroy. "Had
he but the old man's heritage. Ah! he might bring

that into existence which his *belles demoiselles* had
been begging for, ' since many years ; ' a home, — and
such a home, — in the gay city. Here he should tear
down this row of cottages, and make his garden wall ;
there that long rope-walk should give place to vine-
covered arbors ; the bakery yonder should make way
for a costly conservatory ; that wine warehouse should
come down, and the mansion go up. It should be the
finest in the State. Men should never pass it, but they
should say — ' the palace of the De Charleus ; a family
of grand descent, a people of elegance and bounty, a
line as old as France, a fine old man, and seven daughters as beautiful as happy ; whoever dare attempt to
marry there must leave his own name behind him ! '

" The house should be of stones fitly set, brought
down in ships from the land of ' les Yankees,' and it
should have an airy belvedere, with a gilded image tip-
toeing and shining on its peak, and from it you should
see, far across the gleaming folds of the river, the red
roof of Belles Demoiselles, the country-seat. At the
big stone gate there should be a porter's lodge, and it
should be a privilege even to see the ground."

Truly they were a family fine enough, and fancy-
free enough to have fine wishes, yet happy enough
where they were, to have had no wish but to live there
a.ways.

To those, who, by whatever fortune, wandered into
the garden of Belles Demoiselles some summer afternoon as the sky was reddening towards evening, it was
lovely to see the family gathered out upon the tiled
pavement at the foot of the broad front steps, gayly

chatting and jesting, with that ripple of laughter that comes so pleasingly from a bevy of girls. The father would be found seated in their midst, the centre of attention and compliment, witness, arbiter, umpire, critic, by his beautiful children's unanimous appointment, but the single vassal, too, of seven absolute sovereigns.

Now they would draw their chairs near together in eager discussion of some new step in the dance, or the adjustment of some rich adornment. Now they would start about him with excited comments to see the eldest fix a bunch of violets in his button-hole. Now the twins would move down a walk after some unusual flower, and be greeted on their return with the high pitched notes of delighted feminine surprise.

As evening came on they would draw more quietly about their paternal centre. Often their chairs were forsaken, and they grouped themselves on the lower steps, one above another, and surrendered themselves to the tender influences of the approaching night. At such an hour the passer on the river, already attracted by the dark figures of the broad-roofed mansion, and its woody garden standing against the glowing sunset, would hear the voices of the hidden group rise from the spot in the soft harmonies of an evening song; swelling clearer and clearer as the thrill of music warmed them into feeling, and presently joined by the deeper tones of the father's voice; then, as the daylight passed quite away, all would be still, and he would know that the beautiful home had gathered its nestlings under its wings.

And yet, for mere vagary, it pleased them not to be pleased.

"Arti!" called one sister to another in the broad hall, one morning, — mock amazement in her distended eyes, — "something is goin' to took place!"

"*Comm-e-n-t ?*" — long-drawn perplexity.

"Papa is goin' to town!"

The news passed up stairs.

"Inno!" — one to another meeting in a doorway, — "something is goin' to took place!"

"*Qu'est-ce-que c'est!*" — vain attempt at gruffness.

"Papa is goin' to town!"

The unusual tidings were true.   It was afternoon of the same day that the Colonel tossed his horse's bridle to his groom, and stepped up to old Charlie, who was sitting on his bench under a China-tree, his head as was his fashion, bound in a Madras handkerchief The "old man" was plainly under the effect of spirits and smiled a deferential salutation without trusting himself to his feet.

"Eh, well Charlie!" — the Colonel raised his voice to suit his kinsman's deafness, — "how is those times with my friend Charlie?"

"Eh?" said Charlie, distractedly.

"Is that goin' well with my friend Charlie?"

"In de house, — call her," — making a pretence of rising.

"*Non, non!* I don't want," — the speaker paused to breathe — "ow is collection?"

"Oh!" said Charlie, "every day he make me more poorer!"

"What do you hask for it?" asked the planter in-
differently, designating the house by a wave of his
whip.

"Ask for w'at?" said Injin Charlie.

"De *house!* What you ask for it?"

"I don't believe," said Charlie.

"What you would *take* for it!" cried the planter.

"Wait for w'at?"

"What you would *take* for the whole block?"

"I don't want to sell him!"

"I'll give you *ten thousand dollah* for it."

"Ten t'ousand dollah for dis house? Oh, no, dat is
no price. He is blame good old house, — dat old
house." (Old Charlie and the Colonel never swore in
presence of each other.) "Forty years dat old house
didn't had to be paint! I easy can get fifty t'ousand
dollah for dat old house."

"Fifty thousand picayunes; yes," said the Colonel.

"She's a good house. Can make plenty money,"
pursued the deaf man.

"That's what make you so rich, eh, Charlie?"

"*Non,* I don't make nothing. Too blame clever,
me, dat's de troub'. She's a good house, — make
money fast like a steamboat, — make a barrel full in a
week! Me, I lose money all de days. Too blame
clever."

"Charlie!"

"Eh?"

"Tell me what you'll take."

"Make? I don't make *nothing.* Too blame
clever."

" What will you *take?* "

" Oh! I got enough already, — half drunk now."

" What will you take for the 'ouse? "

" You want to buy her? "

" I don't know," — (shrug), — " may*be*, — if you sell it cheap."

" She's a bully old house."

There was a long silence. By and by old Charlie commenced —

" Old Injin Charlie is a low-down dog."

" *C'est vrai, oui!* " retorted the Colonel in an undertone.

" He's got Injin blood in him."

The Colonel nodded assent.

" But he's got some blame good blood, too, ain't it? "

The Colonel nodded impatiently.

" *Bien!* Old Charlie's Injin blood says, 'sell de house, Charlie, you blame old fool!' *Mais*, old Charlie's good blood says, 'Charlie! if you sell dat old house, Charlie, you low-down old dog, Charlie, what de Compte De Charleu make for you grace-gran'-muzzer, de dev' can eat you, Charlie, I don't care.' "

" But you'll sell it anyhow, won't you, old man? "

" No! " And the *no* rumbled off in muttered oaths like thunder out on the Gulf. The incensed old Colonel wheeled and started off.

" Curl! " (Colonel) said Charlie, standing up unsteadily.

The planter turned with an inquiring frown.

" I'll trade with you! " said Charlie.

The Colonel was tempted. " 'Ow'l you trade?" he asked.

" My house for yours ! "

The old Colonel turned pale with anger. He walked very quickly back, and came close up to his kinsman.

" Charlie ! " he said.

" Injin Charlie," — with a tipsy nod.

But by this time self-control was returning. " Sell Belles Demoiselles to you?" he said in a high key, and then laughed " Ho, ho, ho ! " and rode away.

A cloud, but not a dark one, overshadowed the spirits of Belles Demoiselles' plantation. The old master, whose beaming presence had always made him a shining Saturn, spinning and sparkling within the bright circle of his daughters, fell into musing fits, started out of frowning reveries, walked often by himself, and heard business from his overseer fretfully.

No wonder. The daughters knew his closeness in trade, and attributed to it his failure to negotiate for the Old Charlie buildings, — so to call them. They began to depreciate Belles Demoiselles. If a north wind blew, it was too cold to ride. If a shower had fallen, it was too muddy to drive. In the morning the garden was wet. In the evening the grasshopper was a burden. *Ennui* was turned into capital; every headache was interpreted a premonition of ague; and when the native exuberance of a flock of ladies without a want or a care burst out in laughter in the father's face, they spread their French eyes, rolled up their little hands, and with rigid wrists and mock vehe-

mence vowed and vowed again that they only laughed
at their misery, and should pine to death unless they
could move to the sweet city. "Oh! the theatre!
Oh! Orleans Street! Oh! the masquerade! the
Place d'Armes! the ball!" and they would call upon
Heaven with French irreverence, and fall into each
other's arms, and whirl down the hall singing a waltz,
end with a grand collision and fall, and, their eyes
streaming merriment, lay the blame on the slippery
floor, that would some day be the death of the whole
seven.

Three times more the fond father, thus goaded,
managed, by accident, — business accident, — to see
old Charlie and increase his offer; but in vain. He
finally went to him formally.

"Eh?" said the deaf and distant relative. "For
what you want him, eh? Why you don't stay where
you halways be 'appy? Dis is a blame old rat-hole, —
good for old Injin Charlie, — da's all. Why you
don't stay where you be halways 'appy? Why you don't
buy somewheres else?"

"That's none of your business," snapped the
planter. Truth was, his reasons were unsatisfactory
even to himself.

A sullen silence followed. Then Charlie spoke:

"Well, now, look here; I sell you old Charlie's
house."

"*Bien!* and the whole block," said the Colonel.

"Hold on," said Charlie. "I sell you de 'ouse
and de block. Den I go and git drunk, and go to
sleep: de dev' comes along and says, 'Charlie! old

Charlie, you blame low-down old dog, wake up! What you doin' here? Where's de 'ouse what Monsieur le Compte give your grace-gran-muzzer? Don't you see dat fine gentyman, De Charleu, done gone and tore him down and make him over new, you blame old fool, Charlie, you low-down old Injin dog!'"

"I'll give you forty thousand dollars," said the Colonel.

"For de 'ouse?"

"For all."

The deaf man shook his head.

"Forty-five!" said the Colonel.

"What a lie? For what you tell me 'What a lie?' I don't tell you no lie."

"*Non, non!* I give you *forty-five!*" shouted the Colonel.

Charlie shook his head again.

"Fifty!"

He shook it again.

The figures rose and rose to —

"Seventy-five!"

The answer was an invitation to go away and let the owner alone, as he was, in certain specified respects, the vilest of living creatures, and no company for a fine gentyman.

The "fine gentyman" longed to blaspheme, — but before old Charlie! — in the name of pride, how could he? He mounted and started away.

"Tell you what I'll make wid you," said Charlie

The other, guessing aright, turned back without dismounting, smiling.

"How much Belles Demoiselles hoes me now?" asked the deaf one.

"One hundred and eighty thousand dollars," said the Colonel, firmly.

"Yass," said Charlie. "I don't want Belles Demoiselles."

The old Colonel's quiet laugh intimated it made no difference either way.

"But me," continued Charlie, "me,—I'm got le Compte De Charleu's blood in me, any'ow,—a litt' bit, any'ow, ain't it?"

The Colonel nodded that it was.

"*Bien!* If I go out of dis place and don't go to Belles Demoiselles, de peoples will say,—dey will say, 'Old Charlie he been all doze time tell a blame *lie!* He ain't no kin to his old grace-gran-muzzer, not a blame bit! He don't got nary drop of De Charleu blood to save his blame low-down old Injin soul!' No, sare! What I want wid money, den? No, sare! My place for yours!"

He turned to go into the house, just too soon to see the Colonel make an ugly whisk at him with his riding-whip. Then the Colonel, too, moved off.

Two or three times over, as he ambled homeward, laughter broke through his annoyance, as he recalled old Charlie's family pride and the presumption of his offer. Yet each time he could but think better of—not the offer to swap, but the preposterous ancestral loyalty. It was so much better than he could have expected from his "low-down" relative, and not unlike his own whim withal—the proposition which went with it was **forgiven.**

This last defeat bore so harshly on the master of Belles Demoiselles, that the daughters, reading chagrin in his face, began to repent. They loved their father as daughters can, and when they saw their pretended dejection harassing him seriously they restrained their complaints, displayed more than ordinary tenderness, and heroically and ostentatiously concluded there was no place like Belles Demoiselles. But the new mood touched him more than the old, and only refined his discontent. Here was a man, rich without the care of riches, free from any real trouble, happiness as native to his house as perfume to his garden, deliberately, as it were with premeditated malice, taking joy by the shoulder and bidding her be gone to town, whither he might easily have followed, only that the very same ancestral nonsense that kept Injin Charlie from selling the old place for twice its value prevented him from choosing any other spot for a city home.

But by and by the charm of nature and the merry hearts around him prevailed; the fit of exalted sulks passed off, and after a while the year flared up at Christmas, flickered, and went out.

New Year came and passed; the beautiful garden of Belles Demoiselles put on its spring attire; the seven fair sisters moved from rose to rose; the cloud of discontent had warmed into invisible vapor in the rich sunlight of family affection, and on the common memory the only scar of last year's wound was old Charlie's sheer impertinence in crossing the caprice of the De Charleus. The cup of gladness seemed to fill with the filling of the river.

How high that river was! Its tremendous current rolled and tumbled and spun along, hustling the long funeral flotillas of drift,—and how near shore it came! Men were out day and night, watching the levee. On windy nights even the old Colonel took part, and grew light-hearted with occupation and excitement, as every minute the river threw a white arm over the levee's top, as though it would vault over. But all held fast, and, as the summer drifted in, the water sunk down into its banks and looked quite incapable of harm.

On a summer afternoon of uncommon mildness, old Colonel Jean Albert Henri Joseph De Charleu-Marot, being in a mood for revery, slipped the custody of his feminine rulers and sought the crown of the levee, where it was his wont to promenade. Presently he sat upon a stone bench,—a favorite seat. Before him lay his broad-spread fields; near by, his lordly mansion; and being still,—perhaps by female contact,—somewhat sentimental, he fell to musing on his past. It was hardly worthy to be proud of. All its morning was reddened with mad frolic, and far toward the meridian it was marred with elegant rioting. Pride had kept him well-nigh useless, and despised the honors won by valor; gaming had dimmed prosperity; death had taken his heavenly wife; voluptuous ease had mortgaged his lands; and yet his house still stood, his sweet-smelling fields were still fruitful, his name was fame enough; and yonder and yonder, among the trees and flowers, like angels walking in Eden, were the seven goddesses of his only worship.

Just then a slight sound behind him brought him to
his feet. He cast his eyes anxiously to the outer edge
of the little strip of bank between the levee's base and
the river. There was nothing visible. He paused,
with his ear toward the water, his face full of frightened expectation. Ha! There came a single plash-
ing sound, like some great beast slipping into the river,
and little waves in a wide semi-circle came out from
under the bank and spread over the water!

"My God!"

He plunged down the levee and bounded through
the low weeds to the edge of the bank. It was sheer,
and the water about four feet below. He did not
stand quite on the edge, but fell upon his knees a
couple of yards away, wringing his hands, moaning
and weeping, and staring through his watery eyes at a
fine, long crevice just discernible under the matted
grass, and curving outward on either hand toward the
river.

"My God!" he sobbed aloud; "my God!" and
even while he called, his God answered: the tough
Bermuda grass stretched and snapped, the crevice
slowly became a gape, and softly, gradually, with no
sound but the closing of the water at last, a ton or
more of earth settled into the boiling eddy and disappeared.

At the same instant a pulse of the breeze brought
from the garden behind, the joyous, thoughtless laugh
ter of the fair mistresses of Belles Demoiselles.

The old Colonel sprang up and clambered over the
levee. Then forcing himself to a more composed

movement he hastened into the house and ordered his horse.

"Tell my children to make merry while I am gone," he left word. "I shall be back to-night," and the horse's hoofs clattered down a by-road leading to the city.

"Charlie," said the planter, riding up to a window, from which the old man's nightcap was thrust out, "what you say, Charlie,—my house for yours, eh, Charlie—what you say?"

"Ello!" said Charlie; "from where you come from dis time of to-night?"

"I come from the Exchange in St. Louis Street." (A small fraction of the truth.)

"What you want?" said matter-of-fact Charlie.

"I come to trade."

The low-down relative drew the worsted off his ears. "Oh! yass," he said with an uncertain air.

"Well, old man Charlie, what you say: my house for yours,—like you said,—eh, Charlie?"

"I dunno," said Charlie; "it's nearly mine now. Why you don't stay dare youse'f?"

"*Because I don't want!*" said the Colonel savagely. "Is dat reason enough for you? You better take me in de notion, old man, I tell you,—yes!"

Charlie never winced; but how his answer delighted the Colonel! Quoth Charlie:

"I don't care — I take him!—*mais*, possession give right off."

"Not the whole plantation, Charlie; only"—

"I don't care," said Charlie; "we easy can fix dat

Mais, what for you don't want to keep him? I don't want him. You better keep him."

"Don't you try to make no fool of me, old man," cried the planter.

"Oh, no!" said the other. "Oh, no! but you make a fool of yourself, ain't it?"

The dumbfounded Colonel stared; Charlie went on:

"Yass! Belles Demoiselles is more wort' dan tree block like dis one. I pass by dare since two weeks. Oh, pritty Belles Demoiselles! De cane was wave in de wind, de garden smell like a bouquet, de white-cap was jump up and down on de river; seven *belles demoiselles* was ridin' on horses. 'Pritty, pritty, pritty!' says old Charlie. Ah! *Monsieur le père*, 'ow 'appy, 'appy, 'appy!"

"Yass!" he continued — the Colonel still staring — "le Compte De Charleu have two familie. One was low-down Choctaw, one was high up *noblesse*. He gave the low-down Choctaw dis old rat-hole; he give Belles Demoiselles to you gran-fozzer; and now you don't be *satisfait*. What I'll do wid Belles Demoiselles? She'll break me in two years, yass. And what you'll do wid old Charlie's house, eh? You'll tear her down and make you'se'f a blame old fool. I rather wouldn't trade!"

The planter caught a big breathful of anger, but Charlie went straight on:

"I rather wouldn't, *mais* I will do it for you; — ust the same, like Monsieur le Compte would say, 'Charlie, you old fool, I want to shange houses wid you.'"

So long as the Colonel suspected irony he was angry, but as Charlie seemed, after all, to be certainly in earnest, he began to feel conscience-stricken. He was by no means a tender man, but his lately-discovered misfortune had unhinged him, and this strange, un-deserved, disinterested family fealty on the part of Charlie touched his heart. And should he still try to lead him into the pitfall he had dug? He hesitated; — no, he would show him the place by broad daylight, and if he chose to overlook the "caving bank," it would be his own fault; — a trade's a trade.

"Come," said the planter, "come at my house to-night; to-morrow we look at the place before break-fast, and finish the trade."

"For what?" said Charlie.

"Oh, because I got to come in town in the morn-ing."

"I don't want," said Charlie. "How I'm goin' tc come dere?"

"I git you a horse at the liberty stable."

"Well — anyhow — I don't care — I'll go." And they went.

When they had ridden a long time, and were on the road darkened by hedges of Cherokee rose, the Colonel called behind him to the "low-down" scion:

"Keep the road, old man."

"Eh?"

"Keep the road."

"Oh, yes; all right; I keep my word; we don't goin to play no tricks, eh?"

But the Colonel seemed not to hear. His ungenerous design was beginning to be hateful to him. Not only old Charlie's unprovoked goodness was prevailing; the eulogy on Belles Demoiselles had stirred the depths of an intense love for his beautiful home. True, if he held to it, the caving of the bank, at its present fearful speed, would let the house into the river within three months; but were it not better to lose it so, than sell his birthright? Again, — coming back to the first thought, — to betray his own blood! It was only Injin Charlie; but had not the De Charleu blood just spoken out in him? Unconsciously he groaned.

After a time they struck a path approaching the plantation in the rear, and a little after, passing from behind a clump of live-oaks, they came in sight of the villa. It looked so like a gem, shining through its dark grove, so like a great glow-worm in the dense foliage, so significant of luxury and gayety, that the poor master, from an overflowing heart, groaned again.

"What?" asked Charlie.

The Colonel only drew his rein, and, dismounting mechanically, contemplated the sight before him. The high, arched doors and windows were thrown wide to the summer air; from every opening the bright light of numerous candelabra darted out upon the sparkling foliage of magnolia and bay, and here and there in the spacious verandas a colored lantern swayed in the gentle breeze. A sound of revel fell on the ear, the music of harps; and across one window, brighter than the rest, flitted, once or twice, the shadows of dancers. But oh! the shadows flitting across the heart of the fair mansion's master!

"Old Charlie," said he, gazing fondly at his house, "You and me is both old, eh?"

"Yaas," said the stolid Charlie.

"And we has both been bad enough in our time, eh, Charlie?"

Charlie, surprised at the tender tone, repeated "Yaas."

"And you and me is mighty close?"

"Blame close, yaas."

"But you never know me to cheat, old man!"

"No,"—impassively.

"And do you think I would cheat you now?"

"I dunno," said Charlie. "I don't believe."

"Well, old man, old man,"—his voice began to quiver,—"I sha'n't cheat you now. My God!—old man, I tell you—you better not make the trade!"

"Because for what?" asked Charlie in plain anger; but both looked quickly toward the house! The Colonel tossed his hands wildly in the air, rushed forward a step or two, and giving one fearful scream of agony and fright, fell forward on his face in the path. Old Charlie stood transfixed with horror. Belles Demoiselles, the realm of maiden beauty, the home of merriment, the house of dancing, all in the tremor and glow of pleasure, suddenly sunk, with one short, wild wail of terror—sunk, sunk, down, down, down, into the merciless, unfathomable flood of the Mississippi.

Twelve long months were midnight to the mind of the childless father; when they were only half gone,

he took his bed; and every day, and every night, old
Charlie, the "low-down," the "fool," watched him
tenderly, tended him lovingly, for the sake of his
name, his misfortunes, and his broken heart. No
woman's step crossed the floor of the sick-chamber,
whose western dormer-windows overpeered the dingy
architecture of old Charlie's block; Charlie and a
skilled physician, the one all interest, the other all
gentleness, hope, and patience — these only entered
by the door; but by the window came in a sweet-
scented evergreen vine, transplanted from the caving
bank of Belles Demoiselles. It caught the rays of
sunset in its flowery net and let then softly in upon
the sick man's bed; gathered the glancing beams of
the moon at midnight, and often wakened the sleeper
to look, with his mindless eyes, upon their pretty silver fragments strewn upon the floor.

By and by there seemed — there was — a twinkling
dawn of returning reason. Slowly, peacefully, with
an increase unseen from day to day, the light of
reason came into the eyes, and speech became cohe-
rent; but withal there came a failing of the wrecked
body, and the doctor said that monsieur was both
better and worse.

One evening, as Charlie sat by the vine-clad window with his fireless pipe in his hand, the old Colonel's
eyes fell full upon his own, and rested there.

"Charl—," he said with an effort, and his delighted
nurse hastened to the bedside and bowed his best ear.
There was an unsuccessful effort or two, and then he
whispered, smiling with sweet sadness, —

"We didn't trade."

The truth, in this case, was a secondary matter to Charlie; the main point was to give a pleasing answer. So he nodded his head decidedly, as who should say — "Oh yes, we did, it was a bona-fide swap!" but when he saw the smile vanish, he tried the other expedient and shook his head with still more vigor, to signify that they had not so much as approached a bargain; and the smile returned.

Charlie wanted to see the vine recognized. He stepped backward to the window with a broad smile, shook the foliage, nodded and looked smart.

"I know," said the Colonel, with beaming eyes, "— many weeks."

The next day —

"Charl —"

The best ear went down.

"Send for a priest."

The priest came, and was alone with him a whole afternoon. When he left, the patient was very haggard and exhausted, but smiled and would not suffer the crucifix to be removed from his breast.

One more morning came. Just before dawn Charlie, lying on a pallet in the room, thought he was called, and came to the bedside.

"Old man," whispered the failing invalid, "is it caving yet?"

Charlie nodded.

"It won't pay you out."

'Oh, dat makes not'ing," said Charlie. Two big

tears rolled down his brown face. "Dat makes not'in."

The Colonel whispered once more:

"*Mes belles demoiselles!* in paradise; — in the garden — I shall be with them at sunrise;" and so it was.

"Posson Jone'"

"POSSON JONE'."[1]

To Jules St.-Ange — elegant little heathen — there yet remained at manhood a remembrance of having been to school, and of having been taught by a stony-headed Capuchin that the world is round — for example, like a cheese. This round world is a cheese to be eaten through, and Jules had nibbled quite into his cheese-world already at twenty-two.

He realized this as he idled about one Sunday morning where the intersection of Royal and Conti Streets some seventy years ago formed a central corner of New Orleans. Yes, yes, the trouble was he had been wasteful and honest. He discussed the matter with that faithful friend and confidant, Baptiste, his yellow body-servant. They concluded that, papa's patience and *tante's* pin-money having been gnawed away quite to the rind, there were left open only these few easily-enumerated resorts: to go to work — they shuddered; to join Major Innerarity's filibustering expedition; or else — why not? — to try some games of confidence. At twenty-two one must begin to be something. Noth-

[1] Published in Appletons' Journal. Republished by permission.

ing else tempted; could that avail? One could but
try. It is noble to try; and, besides, they were hungry. If one could "make the friendship" of some
person from the country, for instance, with money,
not expert at cards or dice, but, as one would say,
willing to learn, one might find cause to say some
"Hail Marys."

The sun broke through a clearing sky, and Baptiste
pronounced it good for luck. There had been a hurricane in the night. The weed-grown tile-roofs were
still dripping, and from lofty brick and low adobe
walls a rising steam responded to the summer sunlight. Up-street, and across the Rue du Canal, one
could get glimpses of the gardens in Faubourg Ste.-
Marie standing in silent wretchedness, so many tearful
Lucretias, tattered victims of the storm. Short remnants of the wind now and then came down the narrow
street in erratic puffs heavily laden with odors of
broken boughs and torn flowers, skimmed the little
pools of rain-water in the deep ruts of the unpaved
street, and suddenly went away to nothing, like a
juggler's butterflies or a young man's money.

It was very picturesque, the Rue Royale. The rich
and poor met together. The locksmith's swinging key
creaked next door to the bank; across the way,
crouching, mendicant-like, in the shadow of a great im-
porting-house, was the mud laboratory of the mender
of broken combs. Light balconies overhung the rows
of showy shops and stores open for trade this Sunday
morning, and pretty Latin faces of the higher class
glanced over their savagely-pronged railings upon the

passers below. At some windows hung lace curtains, flannel duds at some, and at others only the scraping and sighing one-hinged shutter groaning toward Paris after its neglectful master.

M. St.-Ange stood looking up and down the street for nearly an hour. But few ladies, only the inveter ate mass-goers, were out. About the entrance of the frequent *cafés* the masculine gentility stood leaning on canes, with which now one and now another beckoned to Jules, some even adding pantomimic hints of the social cup.

M. St.-Ange remarked to his servant without turning his head that somehow he felt sure he should soon return those *bons* that the mulatto had lent him.

"What will you do with them?"

"Me!" said Baptiste, quickly; "I will go and see the bull-fight in the Place Congo."

"There is to be a bull-fight? But where is M. Cayetano?"

"Ah, got all his affairs wet in the tornado. Instead of his circus, they are to have a bull-fight — not an ordinary bull-fight with sick horses, but a buffalo-and-tiger fight. I would not miss it" —

Two or three persons ran to the opposite corner, and commenced striking at something with their canes. Others followed. Can M. St.-Ange and servant, who hasten forward — can the Creoles, Cubans, Spaniards, San Domingo refugees, and other loungers — can they hope it is a fight? They hurry forward. Is a man in a fit? The crowd pours in from the side-streets. Have they killed a so-long snake? Bareheaded shopmen leave their wives, who stand upon chairs. The crowd huddles and packs. Those on the outside make little leaps into the air, trying to be tall.

"What is the matter?"

"Have they caught a real live rat?"

"Who is hurt?" asks some one in English.

"*Personne*," replies a shopkeeper; "a man's hat blow' in the gutter; but he has it now. Jules pick' it. See, that is the man, head and shoulders on top the res'."

"He in the homespun?" asks a second shopkeeper.

"Humph! an *Américain* — a West-Floridian; bah!"

"But wait; 'st! he is speaking; listen!"

"To who is he speak ——?"

"Sh-sh-sh! to Jules."

"Jules who?"

"Silence, you! To Jules St.-Ange, what howe me a bill since long time. Sh-sh-sh!"

Then the voice was heard.

Its owner was a man of giant stature, with a slight stoop in his shoulders, as if he was making a constant, good-natured attempt to accommodate himself to ordinary doors and ceilings. His bones were those of an ox. His face was marked more by weather than age, and his narrow brow was bald and smooth. He had instantaneously formed an opinion of Jules St.-Ange, and the multitude of words, most of them lingual curiosities, with which he was rasping the wide-open ears of his listeners, signified, in short, that, as sure as his name was Parson Jones, the little Creole was a plum gentleman."

M. St.-Ange bowed and smiled, and was about to
call attention, by both gesture and speech, to a singular object on top of the still uncovered head, when the
nervous motion of the *Américain* anticipated him, as,
throwing up an immense hand, he drew down a large
roll of bank-notes. The crowd laughed, the West-
Floridian joining, and began to disperse.

"Why, that money belongs to Smyrny Church,"
said the giant.

"You are very dengerous to make your money
expose like that, Misty Posson Jone'," said St.-Ange,
counting it with his eyes.

The countryman gave a start and smile of surprise.

"How d'dyou know my name was Jones?" he
asked; but, without pausing for the Creole's answer,
furnished in his reckless way some further specimens
of West-Floridian English; and the conciseness with
which he presented full intelligence of his home,
family, calling, lodging-house, and present and future
plans, might have passed for consummate art, had it
not been the most run-wild nature. "And I've done
been to Mobile, you know, on busi*ness* for Bethesdy
Church. It's the on'yest time I ever been from home;
now you wouldn't of believed that, would you? But
I admire to have saw you, that's so. You've got to
come and eat with me. Me and my boy ain't been
fed yit. What might one call yo' name? Jools?
Come on, Jools. Come on, Colossus. That's my
niggah — his name's Colossus of Rhodes. Is that yo'
yallah boy, Jools? Fetch him along, Colossus. It

seems like a special provi*dence*. — Jools, do y)u believe in a special provi*dence?* ''

Jules said he did.

The new-made friends moved briskly off, followed by Baptiste and a short, square, old negro, very black and grotesque, who had introduced himself to the mulatto, with many glittering and cavernous smiles, as '' d'body-sarvant of d'Rev'n' Mr. Jones.''

Both pairs enlivened their walk with conversation. Parson Jones descanted upon the doctrine he had mentioned, as illustrated in the perplexities of cotton-growing, and concluded that there would always be '' a special provi*dence* again' cotton untell folks quits a-pressin' of it and haulin' of it on Sundays!''

'' *Je dis*,'' said St.-Ange, in response, '' I thing you is juz right. I believe, me, strong-strong in the im providence, yes. You know my papa he hown a sugah-plantation, you know. 'Jules, me son,' he say one time to me, 'I goin' to make one baril sugah to fedge the moze high price in New Orleans.' Well, he take his bez baril sugah — I nevah see a so careful man like me papa always to make a so beautiful sugah *et sirop*. 'Jules, go at Father Pierre an' ged this lill pitcher fill with holy water, an' tell him sen' his tin bucket, and I will mrke it fill with *quitte.*' I ged the holy-water; my papa sprinkle it over the baril, an' make one cross on the 'ead of the baril.''

'' Why, Jools,'' said Par on Jones, '' that didn't do no good.''

'' Din do no good! Id broughd the so great value! You can strike me dead if thad baril sugah din fedge the more high cost than any other in the city. *Parceque*, the man what buy that baril sugah he make a mistake of one hundred pound" — falling back — "*Mais* certainlee!"

"And you think that was growin' out of the holy-water?" asked the parson.

"*Mais*, what could make it else? Id could not be the *quitte*, because my papa keep the bucket, an' forget to sen' the *quitte* to Father Pierre."

Parson Jones was disappointed.

"Well, now, Jools, you know, I don't think that was right. I reckon you must be a plum Catholic."

M. St.-Ange shrugged. He would not deny his faith.

"I am a *Catholique*, *mais*" — brightening as he hoped to recommend himself anew — "not a good one."

"Well, you know," said Jones — "where's Colossus? Oh! all right. Colossus strayed off a minute in Mobile, and I plum lost him for two days. Here's the place; come in. Colossus and this boy can go to the kitchen. — Now, Colossus, what *air* you a-beckonin' at me faw?"

He let his servant draw him aside and address him in a whisper.

"Oh, go 'way!" said the parson with a jerk. "Who's goin' to throw me? What? Speak louder. Why, Colossus, you shayn't talk so, saw. 'Pon my soul, you're the mightiest fool I ever taken up with. Jest you go down that alley-way with this yalla boy, and don't show yo' face untell yo' called!"

The negro begged; the master wrathily insisted.

"Colossus, will you do ez I tell you, or shell I hev to strike you, saw?"

"O Mahs Jimmy, I—I's gwine; but"—he ventured nearer—"don't on no account drink nothin', Mahs Jimmy."

Such was the negro's earnestness that he put one foot in the gutter, and fell heavily against his master. The parson threw him off angrily.

"Thar, now! Why, Colossus, you most of been dosted with sumthin'; yo' plum crazy.—Humph, come on, Jools, let's eat! Humph! to tell me that when I never taken a drop, exceptin' for chills, in my life—which he knows so as well as me!"

The two masters began to ascend a stair.

"*Mais*, he is a sassy; I would sell him, me," said the young Creole.

"No, I wouldn't do that," replied the parson; "though there is people in Bethesdy who says he is a rascal. He's a powerful smart fool. Why, that boy's got money, Jools; more money than religion, I reckon. I'm shore he fallen into mighty bad company"—they passed beyond earshot.

Baptiste and Colossus, instead of going to the tavern kitchen, passed to the next door and entered the dark rear corner of a low grocery, where, the law notwithstanding, liquor was covertly sold to slaves. There, in the quiet company of Baptiste and the grocer, the colloquial powers of Colossus, which were simply prodigious, began very soon to show themselves.

"For whilst," said he, "Mahs Jimmy has eddica-

tion, you know — whilst he has eddication, I has 'scretion. He has eddication and I has 'scretion, an' so
we gits along."

He drew a black bottle down the counter, and, laying half his length upon the damp board, continued:

"As a p'inciple I discredits de imbimin' of awjus
liquors. De imbimin' of awjus liquors, de wiolut'or
of de Sabbaf, de playin' of de fiddle, and de usin' of
by-words, dey is de fo' sins of de conscience; an' if
any man sin de fo' sins of de conscience, de debble
done sharp his fork fo' dat man. — Ain't that so,
boss?"

The grocer was sure it was so.

"Neberdeless, mind you " — here the orator brimmed
his glass from the bottle and swallowed the contents
with a dry eye — "mind you, a roytious man, sech as
ministers of de gospel and dere body-sarvants, can
take a *leetle* for de weak stomach."

But the fascinations of Colossus's eloquence must
not mislead us; this is the story of a true Christian;
to wit, Parson Jones.

The parson and his new friend ate. But the coffee
M. St.-Ange declared he could not touch; it was too
wretchedly bad. At the French Market, near by,
there was some noble coffee. This, however, would
have to be bought, and Parson Jones had scruples.

"You see, Jools, every man has his conscience to
guide him, which it does so in " —

"Oh, yes!" cried St.-Ange, "conscien'; thad is
the bez, Posson Jone'. Certainlee! I am a *Catho
lique*, you is a *schismatique*; you thing it is wrong to

dring some coffee — well, then, it *is* wrong ; you thing it is wrong to make the sugah to ged the so large price — well, then, it *is* wrong ; I thing it is right — well, then, it *is* right ; it is all 'abit ; *c'est tout.* What a man thing is right, *is right;* 'tis all 'abit. A man muz ncd go again' his conscien'. My faith ! do you thing I would go again' my conscien'? *Mais allons,* led us go and ged some coffee.''

" Jools.''

" W'at?''

"Jools, it ain't the drinkin' of coffee, but the buyin' of it on a Sabbath. You must really excuse me, Jools, it's again' conscience, you know.''

" Ah !'' said St.-Ange, " *c'est* very true. For you it would be a sin, *mais* for me it is only 'abit. Rilligion is a very strange ; I know a man one time, he thing it was wrong to go to cock-fight Sunday evening. I thing it is all 'abit. *Mais,* come, Posson Jone' ; I have got one friend, Miguel ; led us go at his house and ged some coffee. Come ; Miguel have no familie ; only him and Joe — always like to see friend ; *allons,* led us come yonder.''

" Why, Jools, my dear friend, you know,'' said the shamefaced parson, " I never visit on Sundays.''

" Never w'at?'' asked the astounded Creole.

" No,'' said Jones, smiling awkwardly.

" Never visite?''

" Exceptin' sometimes amongst church-members.'' said Parson Jones.

" *Mais,*'' said the seductive St.-Ange, " Miguel and Joe is church-member' — certainlee ! They love to talk about rilligion. Come at Miguel and talk about some rilligion. I am nearly expire for me coffee."

Parson Jones took his hat from beneath his chair and rose up.

"Jools," said the weak giant, "I ought to be in church right now."

"*Mais*, the church is right yonder at Miguel', yes. Ah!" continued St.-Ange, as they descended the stairs, "I thing every man muz have the rilligion he like' the bez — me, I like the *Catholique* rilligion the bez — for me it *is* the bez. Every man will sure go to heaven if he like his rilligion the bez."

"Jools," said the West-Floridian, laying his great hand tenderly upon the Creole's shoulder, as they stepped out upon the *banquette*, "do you think you have any shore hopes of heaven?"

"Yass!" replied St.-Ange; "I am sure-sure. I thing everybody will go to heaven. I thing you will go, *et* I thing Miguel will go, *et* Joe — everybody, I thing — *mais*, hof course, not if they not have been christen'. Even I thing some niggers will go."

"Jools," said the parson, stopping in his walk — "Jools, I *don't* want to lose my niggah."

"You will not loose him. With Baptiste he *cannot* ged loose."

But Colossus's master was not re-assured.

"Now," said he, still tarrying, "this is jest the way; had I of gone to church" —

"Posson Jone'," said Jules.

"What?"

"I tell you. We goin' to church!"

'Will you?" asked Jones, joyously.

"*Allons*, come along," said Jules, taking his elbow.

They walked down the Rue Chartres, passed several corners, and by and by turned into a cross street. The parson stopped an instant as they were turning and looked back up the street.

"W'at you lookin'?" asked his companion.

"I thought I saw Colossus," answered the parson, with an anxious face; "I reckon 'twa'n't him, though." And they went on.

The street they now entered was a very quiet one. The eye of any chance passer would have been at once drawn to a broad, heavy, white brick edifice on the lower side of the way, with a flag-pole standing out like a bowsprit from one of its great windows, and a pair of lamps hanging before a large closed entrance. It was a theatre, honey-combed with gambling-dens. At this morning hour all was still, and the only sign of life was a knot of little barefoot girls gathered within its narrow shade, and each carrying an infant relative. Into this place the parson and M. St.-Ange entered, the little nurses jumping up from the sills to let them pass in.

A half-hour may have passed. At the end of that time the whole juvenile company were laying alternate eyes and ears to the chinks, to gather what they could of an interesting quarrel going on within.

"I did not, saw! I given you no cause of offence, saw! It's not so, saw! Mister Jools simply mistaken the house, thinkin' it was a Sabbath-school! No such thing, saw; I *ain't* bound to bet! Yes, I kin git out

Yes, without bettin'! I hev a right to my opinion; I reckon I'm *a white man*, saw! No saw! I on'y said I didn't think you could get the game on them cards. 'Sno such thing, saw! I do *not* know how to play! I wouldn't hev a rascal's money ef I should win it! Shoot, ef you dare! You can kill me, but you cayn't scare me! No, I shayn't bet! I'll die first! Yes, saw; Mr. Jools can bet for me if he admires to; I ain't his mostah."

Here the speaker seemed to direct his words to St.-Ange.

"Saw, I don't understand you, saw. I never said I'd loan you money to bet for me. I didn't suspicion this from you, saw. No, I won't take any more lemonade; it's the most notorious stuff I ever drank, saw!"

M. St.-Ange's replies were in *falsetto* and not without effect; for presently the parson's indignation and anger began to melt. "Don't ask me, Jools, I can't help you. It's no use; it's a matter of conscience with me, Jools."

"*Mais oui!* 'tis a matt' of conscien' wid me, the same."

"But, Jools, the money's none o' mine, nohow; it belongs to Smyrny, you know."

"If I could make jus' *one* bet," said the persuasive St.-Ange, "I would leave this place, fas'-fas', yes. If I had thing — *mais* I did not soupspicion this from you, Posson Jone'" —

"Don't, Jools, don't!"

"No! Posson Jone'."

"You're bound to win?" said the parson, wavering

"*Mais certainement!* But it is not to win that I want; 'tis me conscien'—me honor!"

"Well, Jools, I hope I'm not a-doin' no wrong. I'll loan you some of this money if you say you'll come right out 'thout takin' your winnin's."

All was still. The peeping children could see the parson as he lifted his hand to his breast-pocket. There it paused a moment in bewilderment, then plunged to the bottom. It came back empty, and fell lifelessly at his side. His head dropped upon his breast, his eyes were for a moment closed, his broad palms were lifted and pressed against his forehead, a tremor seized him, and he fell all in a lump to the floor. The children ran off with their infant-loads, leaving Jules St.-Ange swearing by all his deceased relatives, first to Miguel and Joe, and then to the lifted parson, that he did not know what had become of the money "except if" the black man had got it.

In the rear of ancient New Orleans, beyond the sites of the old rampart, a trio of Spanish forts, where the town has since sprung up and grown old, green with all the luxuriance of the wild Creole summer, lay the Congo Plains. Here stretched the canvas of the historic Cayetano, who Sunday after Sunday sowed the sawdust for his circus-ring.

But to-day the great showman had fallen short of his printed promise. The hurricane had come by night, and with one fell swash had made an irretrievable sop of every thing. The circus trailed away

its bed: aggle.l magnificence, and the ring was cleared
for the bull.

Then the sun seemed to come out and work for the
people. "See," said the Spaniards, looking up at
the glorious sky with its great, white fleets drawn off
upon the horizon — "see — heaven smiles upon the
bull-fight!"

In the high upper seats of the rude amphitheatre sat
the gayly-decked wives and daughters of the Gascons,
from the *métaries* along the Ridge, and the chattering
Spanish women of the Market, their shining hair un-
bonneted to the sun. Next below were their husbands
and lovers in Sunday blouses, milkmen, butchers,
bakers, black-bearded fishermen, Sicilian fruiterers,
swarthy Portuguese sailors, in little woollen caps, and
strangers of the graver sort; mariners of England,
Germany, and Holland. The lowest seats were full of
trappers, smugglers, Canadian *voyageurs*, drinking
and singing; *Américains*, too — more's the shame —
from the upper rivers — who will not keep their seats
— who ply the bottle, and who will get home by and
by and tell how wicked Sodom is; broad-brimmed,
silver-braided Mexicans, too, with their copper cheeks
and bat's eyes. and their tinkling spurred heels. Yonder, in that quieter section, are the quadroon women
in their black lace shawls — and there is Baptiste; and
below them are the turbaned black women, and there
is — but he vanishes — Colossus.

The afternoon is advancing, yet the sport, though
loudly demanded, does not begin. The *Américains*
grow derisive and find pastime in gibes and raillery

They mock the various Latins with their national inflections, and answer their scowls with laughter. Some of the more aggressive shout pretty French greetings to the women of Gascony, and one barge-man, amid peals of applause, stands on a seat and hurls a kiss to the quadroons. The mariners of England, Germany, and Holland, as spectators, like the fun, while the Spaniards look black and cast defiant imprecations upon their persecutors. Some Gascons, with timely caution, pick their women out and depart, running a terrible fire of gallantries.

In hope of truce, a new call is raised for the bull: " The bull, the bull! — hush! "

In a tier near the ground a man is standing and calling — standing head and shoulders above the rest — calling in the *Américaine* tongue. Another man, big and red, named Joe, and a handsome little Creole in elegant dress and full of laughter, wish to stop him, but the flat-boatmen, ha-ha-ing and cheering, will not suffer it. Ah, through some shameful knavery of the men, into whose hands he has fallen, he is drunk! Even the women can see that; and now he throws his arms wildly and raises his voice until the whole great circle hears it. He is preaching!

Ah! kind Lord, for a special providence now! The men of his own nation — men from the land of the open English Bible and temperance cup and song are cheering him on to mad disgrace. And now another call for the appointed sport is drowned by the flat-boatmen singing the ancient tune of Mear. You can hear the words —

" Old Grimes is dead, that good old soul "

— from ribald lips and throats turned brazen with laughter, from singers who toss their hats aloft and roll in their seats; the chorus swells to the accompaniment of a thousand brogans —

> "He used to wear an old gray coat
> All buttoned down before."

A ribboned man in the arena is trying to be heard, and the Latins raise one mighty cry for silence. The big red man gets a hand over the parson's mouth, and the ribboned man seizes his moment.

"They have been endeavoring for hours," he says, "to draw the terrible animals from their dens, but such is their strength and fierceness, that" —

His voice is drowned. Enough has been heard to warrant the inference that the beasts cannot be whipped out of the storm-drenched cages to which menagerie-life and long starvation have attached them, and from the roar of indignation the man of ribbons flies. The noise increases. Men are standing up by hundreds, and women are imploring to be let out of the turmoil. All at once, like the bursting of a dam, the whole mass pours down into the ring. They sweep across the arena and over the showman's barriers. Miguel gets a frightful trampling. Who cares for gates or doors? They tear the beasts' houses bar from bar, and, laying hold of the gaunt buffalo, drag him forth by feet, ears, and tail; and in the midst of the *mêlée*, still head and shoulders above all, wilder, with the cup of the wicked, than any beast, is the man of God from the Florida parishes!

In his arms he bore — and all the people shouted at once when they saw it — the tiger. He had lifted it high up with its back to his breast, his arms clasped under its shoulders; the wretched brute had curled up caterpillar-wise, with its long tail against its belly, and through its filed teeth grinned a fixed and impotent wrath. And Parson Jones was shouting:

"The tiger and the buffler *shell* lay down together! You dah to say they shayn't and I'll comb you with this varmint from head to foot! The tiger and the buffler *shell* lay down together. They *shell!* Now, you, Joe! Behold! I am here to see it done. The lion and the buffler *shell* lay down together!"

Mouthing these words again and again, the parson forced his way through the surge in the wake of the buffalo. This creature the Latins had secured by a lariat over his head, and were dragging across the old rampart and into a street of the city.

The northern races were trying to prevent, and there was pommelling and knocking down, cursing and knife-drawing, until Jules St.-Ange was quite carried away with the fun, laughed, clapped his hands, and swore with delight, and ever kept close to the gallant parson.

Joe, contrariwise, counted all this child's-play an interruption. He had come to find Colossus and the money. In an unlucky moment he made bold to lay hold of the parson, but a piece of the broken barriers in the hands of a flat-boatman felled him to the sod, the terrible crowd swept over him, the lariat was cut and the giant parson hurled the tiger upon the buffalo's back. In another instant both brutes were

dead at the hands of the mob; Jones was lifted from
his feet, and prating of Scripture and the millennium,
of Paul at Ephesus and Daniel in the " buffler's " den,
was borne aloft upon the shoulders of the huzzaing
Américains. Half an hour later he was sleeping
heavily on the floor of a cell in the *calaboza.*

When Parson Jones awoke, a bell was somewhere
tolling for midnight. Somebody was at the door of
his cell with a key. The lock grated, the door swung,
the turnkey looked in and stepped back, and a ray of
moonlight fell upon M. Jules St.-Ange. The prisoner
sat upon the empty shackles and ring-bolt in the centre
of the floor.

" Misty Posson Jone'," said the visitor, softly.

" O Jools ! "

" *Mais,* w'at de matter, Posson Jone' ? "

" My sins, Jools, my sins ! "

" Ah ! Posson Jone', is that something to cry,
because a man get sometime a litt' bit intoxicate?
Mais, if a man keep *all the time* intoxicate, I think
that is again' the conscien'."

" Jools, Jools, your eyes is darkened — oh ! Jools,
where's my pore old niggah ? "

" Posson Jone', never min' ; he is wid Baptiste."

" Where ? "

" I don' know w'ere — *mais* he is wid Baptiste.
Baptiste is a beautiful to take care of somebody."

" Is he as good as you, Jools ? " asked Parson
Jones, sincerely.

Jules was slightly staggered.

" You know, Posson Jone', you know, a nigger

cannot be good as a w'ite man—*mais* Baptiste is a good nigger."

The parson moaned and dropped his chin into his hands.

"I was to of left for home to-morrow, sun-up, on 'he Isabella schooner. Pore Smyrny!" He deeply sighed.

"Posson Jone'," said Jules, leaning against the wall and smiling, "I swear you is the moz funny man I ever see. If I was you I would say, me, 'Ah! 'ow I am lucky! the money I los', it was not mine, any-how!' My faith! shall a man make hisse'f to be the more sorry because the money he los' is not his? Me, I would say, 'it is a specious providence.'

"Ah! Misty Posson Jone'," he continued, "you make a so droll sermon ad the bull-ring. Ha! ha! I swear I thing you can make money to preach thad sermon many time ad the theatre St. Philippe. Hah! you is the moz brave dat I never see, *mais* ad the same time the moz rilligious man. Where I'm goin' to fin' one priest to make like dat? *Mais*, why you can't cheer up an' be 'appy? Me, if I should be mis-erabl' like that I would kill meself."

The countryman only shook his head.

"*Bien*, Posson Jone', I have the so good news for you."

The prisoner looked up with eager inquiry.

"Las' evening when they lock' you, I come right off at M. De Blanc's house to get you let out of de calaboose; M. De Blanc he is the judge. So soon I was entering—'Ah! Jules, me boy, juz the man to make complete the game!' Posson Jone', it was a specious providence! I win in t'ree hours more dan six hundred dollah! Look." He produced a mass of bank-notes, *bons*, and due-bills.

"And you got the pass?" asked the parson, regarding the money with a sadness incomprehensible to Jules.

"It is here; it take the effect so soon the daylight."

"Jools, my friend, your kindness is in vain."

The Creole's face became a perfect blank.

"Because," said the parson, "for two reasons: firstly, I have broken the laws, and ought to stand the penalty; and secondly — you must really excuse me, Jools, you know, but the pass has been got onfairly, I'm afeerd. You told the judge I was innocent; and in neither case it don't become a Christian (which I hope I can still say I am one) to 'do evil that good may come.' I muss stay."

M. St.-Ange stood up aghast, and for a moment speechless, at this exhibition of moral heroism; but an artifice was presently hit upon. "*Mais*, Posson Jone'!" — in his old *falsetto* — "de order — you cannot read it, it is in French — compel you to go hout, sir!"

"Is that so?" cried the parson, bounding up with radiant face — "is that so, Jools?"

The young man nodded, smiling; but, though he smiled, the fountain of his tenderness was opened. He made the sign of the cross as the parson knelt in prayer, and even whispered "Hail Mary, ' etc., quite through, twice over.

Morning broke in summer glory upon a cluster of villas behind the city, nestled under live-oaks and magnolias on the banks of a deep bayou, and known as Suburb St. Jean.

With the first beam came the West-Floridian and the Creole out upon the bank below the village. Upon the parson's arm hung a pair of antique saddle-bags. Baptiste limped wearily behind; both his eyes were encircled with broad, blue rings, and one cheek-bone bore the official impress of every knuckle of Colossus's left hand. The "beautiful to take care of somebody" had lost his charge. At mention of the negro he became wild, and, half in English, half in the "gumbo" dialect, said murderous things. Intimidated by Jules to calmness, he became able to speak confidently on one point; he could, would, and did swear that Colossus had gone home to the Florida parishes; he was almost certain; in fact, he thought so.

There was a clicking of pulleys as the three appeared upon the bayou's margin, and Baptiste pointed out, in the deep shadow of a great oak, the Isabella, moored among the bulrushes, and just spreading her sails for departure. Moving down to where she lay, the parson and his friend paused on the bank, loath to say farewell.

"O Jools!" said the parson, "supposin' Colossus ain't gone home! O Jools, if you'll look him out for me, I'll never forget you — I'll never forget you, nohow, Jools. No, Jools, I never will believe he taken that money. Yes, I know all niggahs will steal" — he set foot upon the gang-plank — "but Colossus wouldn't steal from me. Good-by."

"Misty Posson Jone,'" said St.-Ange, putting his hand on the parson's arm with genuine affection, "hol' on. You see dis money — w'at I win las' night? Well, I win' it by a specious providence, ain't it?"

"There's no tellin'," said the humbled Jones. "Providence

'Moves in a mysterious way
His wonders to perform.'"

"Ah!" cried the Creole, "*c'est* very true. I ged this money in the mysterieuze way. *Mais*, if I keep dis money, you know where it goin' be to-night?"

"I really can't say," replied the parson.

"Goin' to de dev'," said the sweetly-smiling young man.

The schooner-captain, leaning against the shrouds, and even Baptiste, laughed outright.

"O Jools, you mustn't!"

"Well, den, w'at I shall do wid *it* ?"

"Any thing!" answered the parson; "better donate it away to some poor man" —

"Ah! Misty Posson Jone', dat is w'at I want. You los' five hondred dollar' — 'twas me fault."

"No, it wa'n't, Jools."

"*Mais*, it was!"

"No!"

"It *was* me fault! I *swear* it was me fault! *Mais*, here is five hondred dollar'; I wish you shall take it. Here! I don't got no use for money. — Oh, my faith! Posson Jone', you must not begin to cry some more."

Parson Jones was choked with tears. When he found voice he said:

"O Jools, Jools, Jools! my pore, noble, dear, mis-
guidened friend! ef you hed of hed a Christian raisin'!
May the Lord show you your errors better'n I kin,
and bless you for your good intentions — oh, no! I
cayn't touch that money with a ten-foot pole; it wa'n't
rightly got; you must really excuse me, my dear
friend, but I cayn't touch it."

St.-Ange was petrified.

"Good-by, dear Jools," continued the parson.
"I'm in the Lord's haynds, and he's very merciful,
which I hope and trust you'll find it out. Good-by!"
— the schooner swang slowly off before the breeze —
"good-by!"

St.-Ange roused himself.

"Posson Jone'! make me hany'ow *dis* promise: you
never, never, *never* will come back to New Orleans."

"Ah, Jools, the Lord willin', I'll never leave home
again!"

"All right!" cried the Creole; "I thing he's
willin'. Adieu, Posson Jone'. My faith'! you are
the so fighting an' moz rilligious man as I never saw!
Adieu! Adieu!"

Baptiste uttered a cry and presently ran by his master toward the schooner, his hands full of clods.

St.-Ange looked just in time to see the sable form
of Colossus of Rhodes emerge from the vessel's hold,
and the pastor of Smyrna and Bethesda seize him in
his embrace.

"O Colossus! you outlandish old nigger! Thank
the Lord! Thank the Lord!"

The little Creole almost wept. He ran down the

tow-path, laughing and swearing, and making confused allusion to the entire *personnel* and furniture of the lower regions.

By odd fortune, at the moment that St.-Ange further demonstrated his delight by tripping his mulatto into a bog, the schooner came brushing along the reedy bank with a graceful curve, the sails flapped, and the crew fell to poling her slowly along.

Parson Jones was on the deck, kneeling once more in prayer. His hat had fallen before him; behind him knelt his slave. In thundering tones he was confessing himself " a plum fool," from whom " the conceit had been jolted out," and who had been made to see that even his " nigger had the longest head of the two."

Colossus clasped his hands and groaned.

The parson prayed for a contrite heart.

" Oh, yes ! " cried Colossus.

The master acknowledged countless mercies.

" Dat's so ! " cried the slave.

The master prayed that they might still be " piled on."

" Glory ! " cried the black man, clapping his hands ; " pile on ! "

" An' now," continued the parson, " bring this pore, backslidin' jackace of a parson and this pore ole fool nigger back to thar home in peace ! "

" Pray fo' de money ! " called Colossus.

But the parson prayed for Jules.

" Pray fo' de *money !* " repeated the negro.

" And oh, give thy servant back that there lost money ! "

Colossus rose stealthily, and tiptoed by his still shouting master. St.-Ange, the captain, the crew, gazed in silent wonder at the strategist. Pausing but an instant over the master's hat to grin an acknowledgment of his beholders' speechless interest, he softly placed in it the faithfully-mourned and honestly-prayed-for Smyrna fund; then, saluted by the gesticulative, silent applause of St.-Ange and the schoonermen, he resumed his first attitude behind his roaring master.

"Amen!" cried Colossus, meaning to bring him to a close.

"Onworthy though I be" — cried Jones.

"*Amen!*" reiterated the negro.

"A-a-amen!" said Parson Jones.

He rose to his feet, and, stooping to take up his hat, beheld the well-known roll. As one stunned, he gazed for a moment upon his slave, who still knelt with clasped hands and rolling eyeballs; but when he became aware of the laughter and cheers that greeted him from both deck and shore, he lifted eyes and hands to heaven, and cried like the veriest babe. And when he looked at the roll again, and hugged and kissed it, St.-Ange tried to raise a second shout, but choked, and the crew fell to their poles.

And now up runs Baptiste, covered with slime, and prepares to cast his projectiles. The first one fell wide of the mark; the schooner swung round into a long reach of water, where the breeze was in her favor; another shout of laughter drowned the maledictions of the muddy man; the sails filled; Colossus of Rhodes, smiling and bowing as hero of the moment, ducked as the main boom swept round, and the schooner, leaning slightly to the pleasant influence, rustled a moment over the bulrushes, and then sped far away down the rippling bayou.

M. Jules St.-Ange stood long, gazing at the receding vessel as it now disappeared, now re-appeared beyond the tops of the high undergrowth; but, when an arm of the forest hid it finally from sight, he turned townward, followed by that fagged-out spaniel, his servant, saying, as he turned, " Baptiste."

" *Miché?* "

" You know w'at I goin' do wid dis money? "

" *Non, m'sieur.* "

' Well, you can strike me dead if I don't goin' to pay ball my debts! *Allons!* "

He began a merry little song to the effect that his sweetheart was a wine-bottle, and master and man, leaving care behind, returned to the picturesque Rue Royale. The ways of Providence are indeed strange. In all Parson Jones's after-life, amid the many painful reminiscences of his visit to the City of the Plain, the sweet knowledge was withheld from him that by the light of the Christian virtue that shone from him even in his great fall, Jules St.-Ange arose, and went to his father an honest man.

Jean-ah Poquelin

JEAN-AH POQUELIN.

In the first decade of the present century, when the newly established American Government was the most hateful thing in Louisiana — when the Creoles were still kicking at such vile innovations as the trial by jury, American dances, anti-smuggling laws, and the printing of the Governor's proclamation in English — when the Anglo-American flood that was presently to burst in a crevasse of immigration upon the delta had thus far been felt only as slippery seepage which made the Creole tremble for his footing — there stood, a short distance above what is now Canal Street, and considerably back from the line of villas which fringed the river-bank on Tchoupitoulas Road, an old colonial plantation-house half in ruin.

It stood aloof from civilization, the tracts that had once been its indigo fields given over to their first noxious wildness, and grown up into one of the horridest marshes within a circuit of fifty miles.

The house was of heavy cypress, lifted up on pillars, grim, solid, and spiritless, its massive build a strong reminder of days still earlier, when every man had been his own peace officer and the insurrection of

the blacks a daily contingency. Its dark, weather-
beaten roof and sides were hoisted up above the jungly
plain in a distracted way, like a gigantic ammunition-
wagon stuck in the mud and abandoned by some
retreating army. Around it was a dense growth of
low water willows, with half a hundred sorts of thorny
or fetid bushes, savage strangers alike to the "language of flowers" and to the botanist's Greek. They
were hung with countless strands of discolored and
prickly smilax, and the impassable mud below bristled
with *chevaux de frise* of the dwarf palmetto. Two lone
forest-trees, dead cypresses, stood in the centre of the
marsh, dotted with roosting vultures. The shallow
strips of water were hid by myriads of aquatic plants,
under whose coarse and spiritless flowers, could one
have seen it, was a harbor of reptiles, great and small,
to make one shudder to the end of his days.

The house was on a slightly raised spot, the levee
of a draining canal. The waters of this canal did not
run; they crawled, and were full of big, ravening fish
and alligators, that held it against all comers.

Such was the home of old Jean Marie Poquelin, once
an opulent indigo planter, standing high in the esteem
of his small, proud circle of exclusively male acquaintances in the old city; now a hermit, alike shunned by
and shunning all who had ever known him. "The
last of his line," said the gossips. His father lies
under the floor of the St. Louis Cathedral, with the
wife of his youth on one side, and the wife of his old
age on the other. Old Jean visits the spot daily. His
half-brother — alas! there was a mystery; no one

knew what had become of the gentle, young half
brother, more than thirty years his junior, whom once
he seemed so fondly to love, but who, seven years ago,
had disappeared suddenly, once for all, and left no
clew of his fate.

They had seemed to live so happily in each other's
love. No father, mother, wife to either, no kindred
upon earth. The elder a bold, frank, impetuous, chivalric adventurer; the younger a gentle, studious, book-
loving recluse; they lived upon the ancestral estate
like mated birds, one always on the wing, the other
always in the nest.

There was no trait in Jean Marie Poquelin, said the
old gossips, for which he was so well known among his
few friends as his apparent fondness for his "little
brother." "Jacques said this," and "Jacques said
that;" he "would leave this or that, or any thing to
Jacques," for "Jacques was a scholar," and "Jacques
was good," or "wise," or "just," or "far-sighted,"
as the nature of the case required; and "he should
ask Jacques as soon as he got home," since Jacques
was never elsewhere to be seen.

It was between the roving character of the one
brother, and the bookishness of the other, that the
estate fell into decay. Jean Marie, generous gentleman, gambled the slaves away one by one, until none
was left, man or woman, but one old African mute.

The indigo-fields and vats of Louisiana had been
generally abandoned as unremunerative. Certain enterprising men had substituted the culture of sugar;
but while the recluse was too apathetic to take so

active a course, the other saw larger, and, at that
time, equally respectable profits, first in smuggling,
and later in the African slave-trade. What harm
could he see in it? The whole people said it was
vitally necessary, and to minister to a vital public
necessity, — good enough, certainly, and so he laid up
many a doubloon, that made him none the worse in the
public regard.

One day old Jean Marie was about to start upon a
voyage that was to be longer, much longer, than any
that he had yet made. Jacques had begged him hard
for many days not to go, but he laughed him off, and
finally said, kissing him :

" *Adieu, 'tit frère.*"

" No," said Jacques, " I shall go with you."

They left the old hulk of a house in the sole care of
the African mute, and went away to the Guinea coast
together.

Two years after, old Poquelin came home without
his vessel. He must have arrived at his house by
night. No one saw him come. No one saw " his little
brother ; " rumor whispered that he, too, had returned,
but he had never been seen again.

A dark suspicion fell upon the old slave-trader. No
matter that the few kept the many reminded of the
tenderness that had ever marked his bearing to the
missing man. The many shook their heads. " You
know he has a quick and fearful temper ; " and " why
does he cover his loss with mystery?" " Grief would
out with the truth."

" But," said the charitable few, " look in his face ;

see that expression of true humanity.'' The many did look in his face, and, as he looked in theirs, he read the silent question: '' Where is thy brother Abel?'' The few were silenced, his former friends died off, and the name of Jean Marie Poquelin became a symbol o witchery, devilish crime, and hideous nursery fictions.

The man and his house were alike shunned. The snipe and duck hunters forsook the marsh, and the wood-cutters abandoned the canal. Sometimes the hardier boys who ventured out there snake-shooting heard a slow thumping of oar-locks on the canal. They would look at each other for a moment half in con-sternation, half in glee, then rush from their sport in wanton haste to assail with their gibes the unoffend-ing, withered old man who, in rusty attire, sat in the stern of a skiff, rowed homeward by his white-headed African mute.

''O Jean-ah Poquelin! O Jean-ah! Jean-ah Poque-lin!''

It was not necessary to utter more than that. No hint of wickedness, deformity, or any physical or moral demerit; merely the name and tone of mockery: ''Oh, Jean-ah Poquelin!'' and while they tumbled one over another in their needless haste to fly, he would rise carefully from his seat, while the aged mute, with downcast face, went on rowing, and rolling up his brown fist and extending it toward the urchins, would pour forth such an unholy broadside of French impre-cation and invective as would all but craze them with delight.

Among both blacks and whites the house was the

object of a thousand superstitions. Every midnight,
they affirmed, the *feu follet* came out of the marsh and
ran in and out of the rooms, flashing from window to
window. The story of some lads, whose words in ordinary statements were worthless, was generally cred-
ited, that the night they camped in the woods, rather
than pass the place after dark, they saw, about sunset,
every window blood-red, and on each of the four chimneys an owl sitting, which turned his head three times
round, and moaned and laughed with a human voice.
There was a bottomless well, everybody professed to
know, beneath the sill of the big front door under the
rotten veranda ; whoever set his foot upon that threshold disappeared forever in the depth below.

What wonder the marsh grew as wild as Africa !
Take all the Faubourg Ste. Marie, and half the ancient
city, you would not find one graceless dare-devil reckless enough to pass within a hundred yards of the
house after nightfall.

The alien races pouring into old New Orleans began
to find the few streets named for the Bourbon princes
too strait for them. The wheel of fortune, beginning
to whirl, threw them off beyond the ancient corpo-
ration lines, and sowed civilization and even trade
upon the lands of the Graviers and Girods. Fields
became roads, roads streets. Everywhere the leveller
was peering through his glass, rodsmen were whacking
their way through willow-brakes and rose-hedges, and
the sweating Irishmen tossed the blue clay up with
their long-handled shovels.

rather a peaceful and peaceable fearlessness. Across the whole face, not marked in one or another feature, but as it were laid softly upon the countenance like an almost imperceptible veil, was the imprint of some great grief. A careless eye might easily overlook it, but, once seen, there it hung—faint, but unmistakable.

The Governor bowed.

"*Parlez-vous français?*" asked the figure.

"I would rather talk English, if you can do so," said the Governor.

"My name, Jean Poquelin."

"How can I serve you, Mr. Poquelin?"

"My 'ouse is yond'; *dans le marais là-bas.*"

The Governor bowed.

"Dat *marais* billong to me."

"Yes, sir."

"To me; Jean Poquelin; I hown 'im meself."

"Well, sir?"

"He don't billong to you; I get him from me father."

"That is perfectly true, Mr. Poquelin, as far as I am aware."

"You want to make strit pass yond'?"

"I do not know, sir; it is quite probable; but the city will indemnify you for any loss you may suffer—you will get paid, you understand."

"Strit can't pass dare."

"You will have to see the municipal authorities about that, Mr. Poquelin."

A bitter smile came upon the old man's face:

" Ha ! that is all very well," quoth the Jean-Bapt
feeling the reproach of an enterprise that asked nei
co-operation nor advice of them, " but wait till t
come yonder to Jean Poquelin's marsh ; ha ! ha ! ha
The supposed predicament so delighted them, that th
put on a mock terror and whirled about in an assume
stampede, then caught their clasped hands betweel
their knees in excess of mirth, and laughed till the
tears ran ; for whether the street-makers mired in the
marsh, or contrived to cut through old " Jean-ah's "
property, either event would be joyful. Meantime a
line of tiny rods, with bits of white paper in their split
tops, gradually extended its way straight through the
haunted ground, and across the canal diagonally.

"We shall fill that ditch," said the men in mud-
boots, and brushed close along the chained and pad-
locked gate of the haunted mansion. Ah, Jean-ah
Poquelin, those were not Creole boys, to be stampeded
with a little hard swearing.

He went to the Governor. That official scanned the
odd figure with no slight interest. Jean Poquelin was
of short, broad frame, with a bronzed leonine face.
His brow was ample and deeply furrowed. His eye,
large and black, was bold and open like that of a
war-horse, and his jaws shut together with the firm-
ness of iron. He was dressed in a suit of Attakapas
cottonade, and his shirt unbuttoned and thrown back
from the throat and bosom, sailor-wise, showed a her-
culean breast, hard and grizzled. There was no fierceness or defiance in his look, no harsh ungentleness,
no symptom of his unlawful life or violent temper ; but

" *Pardon, Monsieur*, you is not *le Gouverneur?* "

"Yes."

" *Mais*, yes. You har *le Gouverneur*—yes. Veh-well. I come to you. I tell you, strit can't pass at me 'ouse."

"But you will have to see " —

"I come to you. You is *le Gouverneur*. I know not the new laws. I ham a Fr-r-rench-a-man! Fr-rench-a-man have something *aller au contraire*— he come at his *Gouverneur*. I come at you. If me not had been bought from me king like *bossals* in the hold time, ze king gof—France would-a-show *Monsieur le Gouverneur* to take care his men to make strit in right places. *Mais*, I know; we billong to *Monsieur le Président*. I want you do somesin for me, eh?"

"What is it?" asked the patient Governor.

"I want you tell *Monsieur le Président*, strit—can't --pass—at—me—'ouse."

"Have a chair, Mr. Poquelin;" but the old man did not stir. The Governor took a quill and wrote a line to a city official, introducing Mr. Poquelin, and asking for him every possible courtesy. He handed it to him, instructing him where to present it.

"Mr. Poquelin," he said with a conciliatory smile, "tell me, is it your house that our Creole citizens tell such odd stories about?"

The old man glared sternly upon the speaker, and with immovable features said :

"You don't see me trade some Guinea nigga'?"

"Oh, no."

"You don't see me make some smugglin'?"

"No, sir; not at all."

"But, I am Jean Marie Poquelin. I mine me hown bizniss. Dat all right? Adieu."

He put his hat on and withdrew. By and by he stood, letter in hand, before the person to whom it was addressed. This person employed an interpreter.

"He says," said the interpreter to the officer, "he come to make you the fair warning how you muz not make the street pas' at his 'ouse."

The officer remarked that "such impudence was refreshing;" but the experienced interpreter translated freely.

"He says: 'Why you don't want?'" said the interpreter.

The old slave-trader answered at some length.

"He says," said the interpreter, again turning to the officer, "the marass is a too unhealth' for peopl' to live."

"But we expect to drain his old marsh; it's not going to be a marsh."

"*Il dit*" — The interpreter explained in French.

The old man answered tersely.

"He says the canal is a private." said the interpreter.

"Oh! *that* old ditch; that's to be filled up. Tell the old man we're going to fix him up nicely."

Translation being duly made, the man in power was amused to see a thunder-cloud gathering on the old man's face.

"Tell him," he added, "by the time we finish. there'll not be a ghost left in his shanty."

The interpreter began to translate, but —

" *J' comprends, J' comprends,*" said the old man, with an impatient gesture, and burst forth, pouring curses upon the United States, the President, the Territory of Orleans, Congress, the Governor and all his subordinates, striding out of the apartment as he cursed, while the object of his maledictions roared with merriment and rammed the floor with his foot.

" Why, it will make his old place worth ten dollars to one," said the official to the interpreter.

" 'Tis not for de worse of de property," said the interpreter.

" I should guess not," said the other, whittling his chair, — " seems to me as if some of these old Creoles would liever live in a crawfish hole than to have a neighbor."

" You know what make old Jean Poquelin make like that? I will tell you. You know " —

The interpreter was rolling a cigarette, and paused to light his tinder; then, as the smoke poured in a thick double stream from his nostrils, he said, in a solemn whisper :

" He is a witch."

" Ho, ho, ho ! " laughed the other.

" You don't believe it? What you want to bet?" cried the interpreter, jerking himself half up and thrusting out one arm while he bared it of its coatsleeve with the hand of the other. " What you want to bet?"

" How do you know?" asked the official.

" Dass what I goin' to tell you. You know, one

evening I was shooting some *grosbec*. I killed three;
but I had trouble to fine them, it was becoming so
dark. When I have them I start' to come home;
then I got to pas' at Jean Poquelin's house."

"Ho, ho, ho!" laughed the other, throwing his leg
over the arm of his chair.

"Wait," said the interpreter. "I come along slow,
not making some noises; still, still "—

"And scared," said the smiling one.

"*Mais*, wait. I get all pas' the 'ouse. 'Ah!' I
say; 'all right!' Then I see two thing' before!
Hah! I get as cold and humide, and shake like a leaf.
You think it was nothing? There I see, so plain as
can be (though it was making nearly dark), I see Jean
— Marie — Po-que-lin walkin' right in front, and right
there beside of him was something like a man — but
not a man — white like paint!—I dropp' on the grass
from scared — they pass'; so sure as I live 'twas the
ghos' of Jacques Poquelin, his brother!"

"Pooh!" said the listener.

"I'll put my han' in the fire," said the interpreter.

"But did you never think," asked the other,
"that that might be Jack Poquelin, as you call him,
alive and well, and for some cause hid away by his
brother?"

"But there har' no cause!" said the other, and the
entrance of third parties changed the subject.

Some months passed and the street was opened. A
canal was first dug through the marsh, the small one
which passed so close to Jean Poquelin's house was
filled, and the street, or rather a sunny road, just

touched a corner of the old mansion's dooryard. The morass ran dry. Its venomous denizens slipped away through the bulrushes; the cattle roaming freely upon its hardened surface trampled the superabundant undergrowth. The bellowing frogs croaked to westward. Lilies and the flower-de-luce sprang up in the place of reeds; smilax and poison-oak gave way to the purple-plumed iron-weed and pink spiderwort; the bindweeds ran everywhere blooming as they ran, and on one of the dead cypresses a giant creeper hung its green burden of foliage and lifted its scarlet trumpets. Sparrows and red-birds flitted through the bushes, and dewberries grew ripe beneath. Over all these came a sweet, dry smell of salubrity which the place had not known since the sediments of the Mississippi first lifted it from the sea.

But its owner did not build. Over the willow-brakes, and down the vista of the open street, bright new houses, some singly, some by ranks, were prying in upon the old man's privacy. They even settled down toward his southern side. First a wood-cutter's hut or two, then a market gardener's shanty, then a painted cottage, and all at once the faubourg had flanked and half surrounded him and his dried-up marsh.

Ah! then the common people began to hate him. "The old tyrant!" "You don't mean an old *tyrant?*" "Well, then, why don't he build when the public need demands it? What does he live in that unneighborly way for?" "The old pirate!" "The old kidnapper!" How easily even the most

ultra Louisianians put on the imported virtues of the
North when they could be brought to bear against the
hermit. "There he goes, with the boys after him!
Ah! ha! ha! Jean-ah Poquelin! Ah! Jean-ah!
Aha! aha! Jean-ah Marie! Jean-ah Poquelin! The
old villain!" How merrily the swarming Américains
echo the spirit of persecution! "The old fraud,"
they say — " pretends to live in a haunted house, does
he? We'll tar and feather him some day. Guess we
can fix him."

He cannot be rowed home along the old canal now;
he walks. He has broken sadly of late, and the
street urchins are ever at his heels. It is like the
days when they cried : " Go up, thou bald-head," and
the old man now and then turns and delivers ineffectual
curses.

To the Creoles — to the incoming lower class of su-
perstitious Germans, Irish, Sicilians, and others — he
became an omen and embodiment of public and private ill-fortune. Upon him all the vagaries of their
superstitions gathered and grew. If a house caught
fire, it was imputed to his machinations. Did a woman go off in a fit, he had bewitched her. Did a
child stray off for an hour, the mother shivered with
the apprehension that Jean Poquelin had offered him
to strange gods. The house was the subject of every
bad boy's invention who loved to contrive ghostly lies.
" As long as that house stands we shall have bad luck.
Do you not see our pease and beans dying, our cab-
bages and lettuce going to seed and our gardens turning to dust, while every day you can see it raining in

the woods? The rain will never pass old Poquelin's
house. He keeps a fetich. He has conjured the
whole Faubourg St. Marie. And why, the old wretch?
Simply because our playful and innocent children call
after him as he passes."

A "Building and Improvement Company," which
had not yet got its charter, "but was going to," and
which had not, indeed, any tangible capital yet, but
"was going to have some," joined the "Jean-ah Poquelin" war. The haunted property would be such a
capital site for a market-house! They sent a deputation to the old mansion to ask its occupant to sell.
The deputation never got beyond the chained gate and
a very barren interview with the African mute. The
President of the Board was then empowered (for he
had studied French in Pennsylvania and was considered qualified) to call and persuade M. Poquelin to
subscribe to the company's stock; but —

"Fact is, gentlemen," he said at the next meeting,
"it would take us at least twelve months to make Mr.
Pokaleen understand the rather original features of
our system, and he wouldn't subscribe when we'd
done; besides, the only way to see him is to stop him
on the street."

There was a great laugh from the Board; they
couldn't help it. "Better meet a bear robbed of her
whelps," said one.

"You're mistaken as to that," said the President.
"I did meet him, and stopped him, and found him
quite polite. But I could get no satisfaction from
him; the fellow wouldn't talk in French, and when I

spoke in English he hoisted his old shoulders up, and gave the same answer to every thing I said."

"And that was —?" asked one or two, impatient of the pause.

"That it 'don't worse w'ile?'"

One of the Board said: "Mr. President, this market-house project, as I take it, is not altogether a selfish one; the community is to be benefited by it. We may feel that we are working in the public interest [the Board smiled knowingly], if we employ all possible means to oust this old nuisance from among us. You may know that at the time the street was cut through, this old Poquelann did all he could to prevent it. It was owing to a certain connection which I had with that affair that I heard a ghost story [smiles, followed by a sudden dignified check] — ghost story, which, of course, I am not going to relate; but I *may* say that my profound conviction, arising from a prolonged study of that story, is, that this old villain, John Poquelann, has his brother locked up in that old house. Now, if this is so, and we can fix it on him, I merely *suggest* that we can make the matter highly useful. I don't know," he added, beginning to sit down, "but that it is an action we owe to the community — hem!"

"How do you propose to handle the subject?" asked the President.

"I was thinking," said the speaker, "that, as a Board of Directors, it would be unadvisable for us to authorize any action involving trespass; but if you, for instance, Mr. President, should, as it were, for mere curiosity, *request* some one, as, for instance, our excellent Secretary, simply as a personal favor, to look into the matter — this is merely a suggestion.''

The Secretary smiled sufficiently to be understood that, while he certainly did not consider such preposterous service a part of his duties as secretary, he might, notwithstanding, accede to the President's request; and the Board adjourned.

Little White, as the Secretary was called, was a mild, kind-hearted little man, who, nevertheless, had no fear of any thing, unless it was the fear of being unkind.

'' I tell you frankly,'' he privately said to the President, '' I go into this purely for reasons of my own.''

The next day, a little after nightfall, one might have descried this little man slipping along the rear fence of the Poquelin place, preparatory to vaulting over into the rank, grass-grown yard, and bearing himself altogether more after the manner of a collector of rare chickens than according to the usage of secretaries.

The picture presented to his eye was not calculated to enliven his mind. The old mansion stood out against the western sky, black and silent. One long, lurid pencil-stroke along a sky of slate was all that was left of daylight. No sign of life was apparent; no light at any window, unless it might have been on the side of the house hidden from view. No owls were on the chimneys, no dogs were in the yard.

He entered the place, and ventured up behind a small cabin which stood apart from the house. Through one of its many crannies he easily detected the African mute crouched before a flickering pine-knot, his head on his knees, fast asleep.

He concluded to enter the mansion, and, with that view, stood and scanned it. The broad rear steps of the veranda would not serve him; he might meet some one midway. He was measuring, with his eye, the proportions of one of the pillars which supported it, and estimating the practicability of climbing it, when he heard a footstep. Some one dragged a chair out toward the railing, then seemed to change his mind and began to pace the veranda, his footfalls resounding on the dry boards with singular loudness. Little White drew a step backward, got the figure between himself and the sky, and at once recognized the short, broad-shouldered form of old Jean Poquelin.

He sat down upon a billet of wood, and, to escape the stings of a whining cloud of mosquitoes, shrouded his face and neck in his handkerchief, leaving his eyes uncovered.

He had sat there but a moment when he noticed a strange, sickening odor, faint, as if coming from a distance, but loathsome and horrid.

Whence could it come? Not from the cabin; not from the marsh, for it was as dry as powder. It was not in the air; it seemed to come from the ground.

Rising up, he noticed, for the first time, a few steps before him a narrow footpath leading toward the house. He glanced down it — ha! right there was some one coming — ghostly white!

Quick as thought, and as noiselessly, he lay down at

full length against the cabin. It was bold strategy, and yet, there was no denying it, little White felt that he was frightened. "It is not a ghost," he said to himself. "I *know* it cannot be a ghost;" but the perspiration burst out at every pore, and the air seemed to thicken with heat. "It is a living man," he said in his thoughts. "I hear his footstep, and I hear old Poquelin's footsteps, too, separately, over on the veranda. I am not discovered; the thing has passed; there is that odor again; what a smell of death! Is it coming back? Yes. It stops at the door of the cabin. Is it peering in at the sleeping mute? It moves away. It is in the path again. Now it is gone." He shuddered. "Now, if I dare venture, the mystery is solved." He rose cautiously, close against the cabin, and peered along the path.

The figure of a man, a presence if not a body — but whether clad in some white stuff or naked the darkness would not allow him to determine — had turned, and now, with a seeming painful gait, moved slowly from him. "Great Heaven! can it be that the dead do walk?" He withdrew again the hands which had gone to his eyes. The dreadful object passed between two pillars and under the house. He listened. There was a faint sound as of feet upon a staircase; then all was still except the measured tread of Jean Poquelin walking on the veranda, and the heavy respirations of the mute slumbering in the cabin.

The little Secretary was about to retreat; but as he looked once more toward the haunted house a dim light appeared in the crack of a closed window, and presently old Jean Poquelin came, dragging his chair, and sat down close against the shining cranny. He spoke in a low, tender tone in the French tongue, making some inquiry. An answer came from within. Was it the voice of a human? So unnatural was it — so hollow, so discordant, so unearthly — that the stealthy listener shuddered again from head to foot, and when something stirred in some bushes near by — though it may have been nothing more than a rat — and came scuttling through the grass, the little Secretary actually turned and fled. As he left the enclosure he moved with bolder leisure through the bushes; yet now and then he spoke aloud: "Oh, oh! I see, I understand!" and shut his eyes in his hands.

How strange that henceforth little White was the champion of Jean Poquelin! In season and out of season — wherever a word was uttered against him — the Secretary, with a quiet, aggressive force that instantly arrested gossip, demanded upon what authority the statement or conjecture was made; but as he did not condescend to explain his own remarkable attitude, it was not long before the disrelish and suspicion which had followed Jean Poquelin so many years fell also upon him.

It was only the next evening but one after his adventure that he made himself a source of sullen amazement to one hundred and fifty boys, by ordering them to desist from their wanton hallooing. Old Jean Poquelin, standing and shaking his cane, rolling out his long-drawn maledictions, paused and stared, then gave the Secretary a courteous bow and started on.

The boys, save one, from pure astonishment, ceased but a ruffianly little Irish lad, more daring than any had yet been, threw a big hurtling clod, that struck old Poquelin between the shoulders and burst like a shell. The enraged old man wheeled with uplifted staff to give chase to the scampering vagabond; and — he may have tripped, or he may not, but he fell full length. Little White hastened to help him up, but he waved him off with a fierce imprecation and staggering to his feet resumed his way homeward. His lips were reddened with blood.

Little White was on his way to the meeting of the Board. He would have given all he dared spend to have staid away, for he felt both too fierce and too tremulous to brook the criticisms that were likely to be made.

"I can't help it, gentlemen; I can't help you to make a case against the old man, and I'm not going to."

"We did not expect this disappointment, Mr. White."

"I can't help that, sir. No, sir; you had better not appoint any more investigations. Somebody'll investigate himself into trouble. No, sir; it isn't a threat, it is only my advice, but I warn you that whoever takes the task in hand will rue it to his dying day — which may be hastened, too."

The President expressed himself "surprised."

"I don't care a rush," answered little White, wildly and foolishly. "I don't care a rush if you are, sir. No, my nerves are not disordered; my head's as clear as a bell. No, I'm *not* excited."

A Director remarked that the Secretary looked as though he had waked from a nightmare.

"Well, sir, if you want to know the fact, I have; and if you choose to cultivate old Poquelin's society you can have one, too."

"White," called a facetious member, but White did not notice. "White," he called again.

"What?" demanded White, with a scowl.

"Did you see the ghost?"

"Yes, sir; I did," cried White, hitting the table, and handing the President a paper which brought the Board to other business.

The story got among the gossips that somebody (they were afraid to say little White) had been to the Poquelin mansion by night and beheld something appalling. The rumor was but a shadow of the truth, magnified and distorted as is the manner of shadows. He had seen skeletons walking, and had barely escaped the clutches of one by making the sign of the cross.

Some madcap boys with an appetite for the horrible plucked up courage to venture through the dried marsh by the cattle-path, and come before the house at a spectral hour when the air was full of bats. Something which they but half saw—half a sight was enough—sent them tearing back through the willow-brakes and acacia bushes to their homes, where they fairly dropped down, and cried:

"Was it white?" "No—yes—nearly so—we can't tell—but we saw it." And one could hardly doubt, to look at their ashen faces, that they had, whatever it was.

"If that old rascal lived in the country we come from," said certain Américains, "he'd have been tarred and feathered before now, wouldn't he, Sanders?"

"Well, now he just would."

"And we'd have rid him on a rail, wouldn't we?"

"That's what I allow."

"Tell you what you *could* do." They were talking to some rollicking Creoles who had assumed an absolute necessity for doing *something*. "What is it you call this thing where an old man marries a young girl, and you come out with horns and" —

"*Charivari?*" asked the Creoles.

"Yes, that's it. Why don't you shivaree him?" Felicitous suggestion.

Little White, with his wife beside him, was sitting on their doorsteps on the sidewalk, as Creole custom had taught them, looking toward the sunset. They had moved into the lately-opened street. The view was not attractive on the score of beauty. The houses were small and scattered, and across the flat commons, spite of the lofty tangle of weeds and bushes, and spite of the thickets of acacia, they needs must see the dismal old Poquelin mansion, tilted awry and shutting out the declining sun. The moon, white and slender, was hanging the tip of its horn over one of the chimneys.

"And you say," said the Secretary, "the old black man has been going by here alone? Patty, suppose old Poquelin should be concocting some mischief; he don't lack provocation; the way that clod hit him the other day was enough to have killed him. Why, Patty, he dropped as quick as *that!* No wonder you haven't seen him. I wonder if they haven't heard something about him up at the drug-store. Suppose I go and see."

"Do," said his wife.

She sat alone for half an hour, watching that sudden going out of the day peculiar to the latitude.

"That moon is ghost enough for one house," she said, as her husband returned. "It has gone right down the chimney."

"Patty," said little White, "the drug-clerk says the boys are going to shivaree old Poquelin to-night. I'm going to try to stop it."

"Why, White," said his wife, "you'd better not. You'll get hurt."

"No, I'll not."

"Yes, you will."

"I'm going to sit out here until they come along. They're compelled to pass right by here."

"Why, White, it may be midnight before they start ; you're not going to sit out here till then."

"Yes, I am."

"Well, you're very foolish," said Mrs. White in an undertone, looking anxious, and tapping one of the steps with her foot.

They sat a very long time talking over little family matters.

"What's that?" at last said Mrs. White.

"That's the nine-o'clock gun," said White, and they relapsed into a long-sustained, drowsy silence.

"Patty, you'd better go in and go to bed," said he at last.

"I'm not sleepy."

"Well, you're very foolish," quietly remarked little White, and again silence fell upon them.

"Patty, suppose I walk out to the old house and see if I can find out any thing."

"Suppose," said she, "you don't do any such — listen!"

Down the street arose a great hubbub. Dogs and boys were howling and barking; men were laughing, shouting, groaning, and blowing horns, whooping, and clanking cow-bells, whinnying, and howling, and rattling pots and pans.

"They are coming this way," said little White. "You had better go into the house, Patty."

"So had you."

"No. I'm going to see if I can't stop them."

"Why, White!"

"I'll be back in a minute," said White, and went toward the noise.

In a few moments the little Secretary met the mob. The pen hesitates on the word, for there is a respectable difference, measurable only on the scale of the half century, between a mob and a *charivari*. Little White lifted his ineffectual voice. He faced the head of the disorderly column, and cast himself about as if he were made of wood and moved by the jerk of a string. He rushed to one who seemed, from the size and clatter of his tin pan, to be a leader. "*Stop these fellows, Bienvenu, stop them just a minute, till I tell them*

something." Bienvenu turned and brandished his in-
struments of discord in an imploring way to the crowd.
They slackened their pace, two or three hushed their
horns and joined the prayer of little White and Bienvenu for silence. The throng halted. The hush was
delicious.

"Bienvenu," said little White, "don't shivaree old
Poquelin to-night; he's " —

"My fwang," said the swaying Bienvenu, "who
tail you I goin' to chahivahi somebody, eh? You sink
bickause I make a little playfool wiz zis tin pan zat I
am *dhonk?*"

"Oh, no, Bienvenu, old fellow, you're all right. I
was afraid you might not know that old Poquelin was
sick, you know, but you're not going there, are you?"

"My fwang, I vay soy to tail you zat you ah dhonk
as de dev'. I am *shem* of you. I ham ze servan' of
ze *publique*. Zese *citoyens* goin' to wickwest Jean
Poquelin to give to the Ursuline' two hondred fifty
dolla' " —

"*Hé quoi!*" cried a listener, "*Cinq cent piastres,
oui!*"

"*Oui!*" said Bienvenu, "and if he wiffuse we make
him some lit' *musique;* ta-ra ta!" He hoisted a
merry hand and foot, then frowning, added: "Old
Poquelin got no bizniz dhink s'much w'isky."

"But, gentlemen," said little White, around whom
a circle had gathered, "the old man is very sick."

"My faith!" cried a tiny Creole, "we did not make
him to be sick. W'en we have say we going make la
charivari, do you want that we hall tell a lie? My
faith! 'sfools!"

"But you can shivaree somebody else," said desperate little White.

"*Oui!*" cried Bienvenu, "*et chahivahi* Jean-ah Poquelin tomo'w!'"

"Let us go to Madame Schneider!'" cried two or three, and amid huzzas and confused cries, among which was heard a stentorian Celtic call for drinks, the crowd again began to move.

"*Cent piastres pour l'hôpital de charité!*"

"Hurrah!'"

"One hongred dolla' for Charity Hospital!'"

"Hurrah!'"

"Whang!'" went a tin pan, the crowd yelled, and Pandemonium gaped again. They were off at a right angle.

Nodding, Mrs. White looked at the mantle-clock.

"Well, if it isn't away after midnight."

The hideous noise down street was passing beyond earshot. She raised a sash and listened. For a moment there was silence. Some one came to the door.

"Is that you, White?"

"Yes." He entered. "I succeeded, Patty."

"Did you?" said Patty, joyfully.

"Yes. They've gone down to shivaree the old Dutchwoman who married her step-daughter's sweetheart. They say she has got to pay a hundred dollars to the hospital before they stop."

The couple retired, and Mrs. White slumbered. She was awakened by her husband snapping the lid of his watch.

"What time?" she asked.

" Half-past three. Patty, I haven't slept a wink.
Those fellows are out yet. Don't you hear them?"

" Why, White, they're coming this way!"

" I know they are," said White, sliding out of bed
and drawing on his clothes, " and they're coming fast.
You'd better go away from that window, Patty. My!
what a clatter!"

" Here they are," said Mrs. White, but her husband was gone. Two or three hundred men and boys
pass the place at a rapid walk straight down the broad,
new street, toward the hated house of ghosts. The
din was terrific. She saw little White at the head of
the rabble brandishing his arms and trying in vain to
make himself heard; but they only shook their heads
laughing and hooting the louder, and so passed, bearing him on before them.

Swiftly they pass out from among the houses, away
from the dim oil lamps of the street, out into the
broad starlit commons, and enter the willowy jungles
of the haunted ground. Some hearts fail and their
owners lag behind and turn back, suddenly remember-
ing how near morning it is. But the most part push
on, tearing the air with their clamor.

Down ahead of them in the long, thicket-darkened
way there is — singularly enough — a faint, dancing
light. It must be very near the old house; it is. It
has stopped now. It is a lantern, and is under a well-
known sapling which has grown up on the wayside
since the canal was filled. Now it swings mysteriously
to and fro. A goodly number of the more ghost-
fearing give up the sport; but a full hundred move

orward at a run, doubling their devilish howling and banging.

Yes; it is a lantern, and there are two persons under the tree. The crowd draws near — drops into a walk; one of the two is the old African mute; he lifts the lantern up so that it shines on the other; the crowd recoils; there is a hush of all clangor, and all at once, with a cry of mingled fright and horror from every throat, the whole throng rushes back, dropping every thing, sweeping past little White and hurrying on, never stopping until the jungle is left behind, and then to find that not one in ten has seen the cause of the stampede, and not one of the tenth is certain what it was.

There is one huge fellow among them who looks capable of any villany. He finds something to mount on, and, in the Creole *patois*, calls a general halt. Bienvenu sinks down, and, vainly trying to recline gracefully, resigns the leadership. The herd gather round the speaker; he assures them that they have been outraged. Their right peaceably to traverse the public streets has been trampled upon. Shall such encroachments be endured? It is now daybreak. Let them go now by the open light of day and force a free passage of the public highway!

A scattering consent was the response, and the crowd, thinned now and drowsy, straggled quietly down toward the old house. Some drifted ahead, others sauntered behind, but every one, as he again neared the tree, came to a stand-still. Little White sat upon a bank of turf on the opposite side of the way looking very stern and sad. To each new-comer he put the same question:

"Did you come here to go to old Poquelin's?"

"Yes."

"He's dead." And if the shocked hearer started away he would say: "Don't go away."

"Why not?"

"I want you to go to the funeral presently."

If some Louisianian, too loyal to dear France or Spain to understand English, looked bewildered, some one would interpret for him; and presently they went. Little White led the van, the crowd trooping after him down the middle of the way. The gate, that had never been seen before unchained, was open. Stern little White stopped a short distance from it; the rabble stopped behind him. Something was moving out from under the veranda. The many whisperers stretched upward to see. The African mute came very slowly toward the gate, leading by a cord in the nose a small brown bull, which was harnessed to a rude cart. On the flat body of the cart, under a black cloth, were seen the outlines of a long box.

"Hats off, gentlemen," said little White, as the box came in view, and the crowd silently uncovered.

"Gentlemen," said little White, "here come the last remains of Jean Marie Poquelin, a better man, I'm afraid, with all his sins, — yes a better — a kinder man to his blood — a man of more self-forgetful goodness — than all of you put together will ever dare to be."

There was a profound hush as the vehicle came

creaking through the gate; but when it turned away from them toward the forest, those in front started suddenly. There was a backward rush, then all stood still again staring one way; for there, behind the bier, with eyes cast down and labored step, walked the living remains — all that was left — of little Jacques Poquelin, the long-hidden brother — a leper, as white as snow

Dumb with horror, the cringing crowd gazed upon the walking death. They watched, in silent awe, the slow *cortége* creep down the long, straight road and lessen on the view, until by and by it stopped where a wild, unfrequented path branched off into the undergrowth toward the rear of the ancient city.

"They are going to the *Terre aux Lépreux*," said one in the crowd. The rest watched them in silence.

The little bull was set free; the mute, with the strength of an ape, lifted the long box to his shoulder. For a moment more the mute and the leper stood in sight, while the former adjusted his heavy burden; then, without one backward glance upon the unkind human world, turning their faces toward the ridge in the depths of the swamp known as the Leper's Land, they stepped into the jungle, disappeared, and were never seen again.

'Tite Poulette

'TITE POULETTE.

KRISTIAN KOPPIG was a rosy-faced, beardless young Dutchman. He was one of that army of gentlemen who, after the purchase of Louisiana, swarmed from all parts of the commercial world, over the mountains of Franco-Spanish exclusiveness, like the Goths over the Pyrenees, and settled down in New Orleans to pick up their fortunes, with the diligence of hungry pigeons. He may have been a German; the distinction was too fine for Creole haste and disrelish.

He made his home in a room with one dormer window looking out, and somewhat down, upon a building opposite, which still stands, flush with the street, a century old. Its big, round-arched windows in a long, second-story row, are walled up, and two or three from time to time have had smaller windows let into them again, with odd little latticed peep-holes in their batten shutters. This had already been done when Kristian Koppig first began to look at them from his solitary dormer window.

All the features of the building lead me to guess that it is a remnant of the old Spanish Barracks, whose extensive structure fell by government sale into

213

private hands a long time ago. At the end toward the swamp a great, oriental-looking passage is left, with an arched entrance, and a pair of ponderous wooden doors. You look at it, and almost see Count O'Reilly's artillery come bumping and trundling out, and dash around into the ancient Plaza to bang away at King St. Charles's birthday.

I do not know who lives there now. You might stand about on the opposite *banquette* for weeks and never find out. I suppose it is a residence, for it does not look like one. That is the rule in that region.

In the good old times of duels, and bagatelle-clubs, and theatre-balls, and Cayetano's circus, Kristian Koppig rooming as described, there lived in the portion of this house, partly overhanging the archway, a palish handsome woman, by the name — or going by the name — of Madame John. You would hardly have thought of her being " colored." Though fading, she was still of very attractive countenance, fine, rather severe features, nearly straight hair carefully kept, and that vivid black eye so peculiar to her kind. Her smile, which came and went with her talk, was sweet and exceedingly ir telligent; and something told you, as you looked at her, that she was one who had had to learn a great deal in this troublesome life.

" But ! " — the Creole lads in the street would say — " — her daughter ! " and there would be lifting of arms, wringing of fingers, rolling of eyes, rounding of mouths, gaspings and clasping of hands. " So beautiful, beautiful, beautiful ! White ? — white like a water lily ! White — like a magnolia ! "

Applause would follow, and invocation of all the saints to witness.

And she could sing.

"Sing?" (disdainfully) — "if a mocking-bird can *sing!* Ha!"

They could not tell just how old she was; they "would give her about seventeen."

Mother and daughter were very fond. The neighbors could hear them call each other pet names, and see them sitting together, sewing, talking happily to each other in the unceasing French way, and see them go out and come in together on their little tasks and errands. "'Tite Poulette," the daughter was called; she never went out alone.

And who was this Madame John?

"Why, you know! — she was" — said the wig-maker at the corner to Kristian Koppig — "I'll tell you. You know? — she was" — and the rest atomized off in a rasping whisper. She was the best yellow-fever nurse in a thousand yards round; but that is not what the wig-maker said.

A block nearer the river stands a house altogether different from the remnant of old barracks. It is of frame, with a deep front gallery over which the roof extends. It has become a den of Italians, who sell fuel by daylight, and by night are up to no telling what extent of deviltry. This was once the home of a gay gentleman, whose first name happened to be John. He was a member of the Good Children Social Club. As his parents lived with him, his wife would, according to custom, have been called Madame John·

but he had no wife. His father died, then his mother; last of all, himself. As he is about to be off, in comes Madame John, with 'Tite Poulette, then an infant, on her arm.

"Zalli," said he, "I am going."

She bowed her head, and wept.

"You have been very faithful to me, Zalli."

She wept on.

"Nobody to take care of you now, Zalli."

Zalli only went on weeping.

"I want to give you this house, Zalli; it is for you and the little one."

An hour after, amid the sobs of Madame John, she and the "little one" inherited the house, such as it was. With the fatal caution which characterizes ignorance, she sold the property and placed the proceeds in a bank, which made haste to fail. She put on widow's weeds, and wore them still when 'Tite Poulette "had seventeen," as the frantic lads would say.

How they did chatter over her. Quiet Kristian Koppig had never seen the like. He wrote to his mother, and told her so. A pretty fellow at the corner would suddenly double himself up with beckoning to a knot of chums; these would hasten up; recruits would come in from two or three other directions; as they reached the corner their countenances would quickly assume a genteel severity, and presently, with her mother, 'Tite Poulette would pass — tall, straight, lithe, her great black eyes made tender by their sweeping lashes, the faintest tint of color in her Southern cheek, her form all grace, her carriage a wonder of simple dignity.

The instant she was gone every tongue was let slip on the marvel of her beauty; but, though theirs were only the loose New Orleans morals of over fifty years ago, their unleashed tongues never had attempted any greater liberty than to take up the pet name, 'Tite Poulette. And yet the mother was soon to be, as we shall discover, a paid dancer at the *Salle de Condé*.

To Zalli, of course, as to all "quadroon ladies," the festivities of the Conde-street ball-room were familiar of old. There, in the happy days when dear Monsieur John was young, and the eighteenth century old, she had often repaired under guard of her mother — dead now, alas! — and Monsieur John would slip away from the dull play and dry society of Théâtre d'Orléans, and come around with his crowd of elegant friends; and through the long sweet hours of the ball she had danced, and laughed, and coquetted under her satin mask, even to the baffling and tormenting of that prince of gentlemen, dear Monsieur John himself. No man of questionable blood dare set his foot within the door. Many noble gentlemen were pleased to dance with her. Colonel De —— and General La ——: city councilmen and officers from the Government House. There were no paid dancers then. Every thing was decorously conducted indeed! Every girl's mother was there, and the more discreet always left before there was too much drinking. Yes, it was gay, gay! — but sometimes dangerous. Ha! more times than a few had Monsieur John knocked down some long-haired and long-knifed rowdy, and kicked the breath out of him for looking saucily at her; but that was like him, he was so brave and kind;—and he is gone!

There was no room for widow's weeds there. So when she put these on, her glittering eyes never again looked through her pink and white mask, and she was glad of it; for never, never in her life had they so looked for anybody but her dear Monsieur John, and now he was in heaven—so the priest said—and she was a sick-nurse.

Living was hard work; and, as Madame John had been brought up tenderly, and had done what she could to rear her daughter in the same mistaken way, with, of course, no more education than the ladies in society got, they knew nothing beyond a little music and embroidery. They struggled as they could, faintly; now giving a few private dancing lessons, now dressing hair, but ever beat back by the steady detestation of their imperious patronesses; and, by and by, for want of that priceless worldly grace known among the flippant as "money-sense," these two poor children, born of misfortune and the complacent badness of the times, began to be in want.

Kristian Koppig noticed from his dormer window one day a man standing at the big archway opposite, and clanking the brass knocker on the wicket that was in one of the doors. He was a smooth man, with his hair parted in the middle, and his cigarette poised on a tiny gold holder. He waited a moment, politely cursed the dust, knocked again, threw his slender sword-cane under his arm, and wiped the inside of his hat with his handkerchief.

Madame John held a parley with him at the wicket. 'Tite Poulette was nowhere seen. He stood at the gate while Madame John went up-stairs. Kristian Koppig knew him. He knew him as one knows a snake. He was the manager of the *Salle de Condé* Presently Madame John returned with a little bundle, and they hurried off together.

And now what did this mean? Why, by any one of ordinary acuteness the matter was easily understood, but, to tell the truth, Kristian Koppig was a trifle dull, and got the idea at once that some damage was being planned against 'Tite Poulette. It made the gentle Dutchman miserable not to be minding his own busi ness, and yet —

"But the woman certainly will not attempt" — said he to himself — "no, no! she cannot." Not being able to guess what he meant, I cannot say whether she could or not. I know that next day Kristian Koppig, glancing eagerly over the "*Ami des Lois*," read an advertisement which he had always before skipped with a frown. It was headed, "*Salle de Condé*," and, being interpreted, signified that a new dance was to be introduced, the *Danse de Chinois*, and that *a young lady* would follow it with the famous "*Danse du Shawl*."

It was the Sabbath. The young man watched the opposite window steadily and painfully from early in the afternoon until the moon shone bright; and from the time the moon shone bright until Madame John! — joy! — Madame John! and not 'Tite Poulette, stepped through the wicket, much dressed and well muffled.

and hurried off toward the *Rue Condé.* Madame John was the "young lady;" and the young man's mind, glad to return to its own unimpassioned affairs, relapsed into quietude.

Madame John danced beautifully. It had to be done. It brought some pay, and pay was bread; and every Sunday evening, with a touch here and there of paint and powder, the mother danced the dance of the shawl, the daughter remaining at home alone.

Kristian Koppig, simple, slow-thinking young Dutchman, never noticing that he staid at home with his window darkened for the very purpose, would see her come to her window and look out with a little wild, alarmed look in her magnificent eyes, and go and come again, and again, until the mother, like a storm-driven bird, came panting home.

Two or three months went by.

One night, on the mother's return, Kristian Koppig coming to his room nearly at the same moment, there was much earnest conversation, which he could see, but not hear.

" 'Tite Poulette," said Madame John, "you are seventeen."

"True, Maman."

"Ah! my child, I see not how you are to meet the future." The voice trembled plaintively.

"But how, Maman?"

"Ah! you are not like others; no fortune, no pleasure, no friend."

"Maman!"

"No, no; — I thank God for it; I am glad you are

not; but you will be lonely, lonely, all your poor life long. There is no place in this world for us poor women. I wish that we were either white or black!" —and the tears, two "shining ones," stood in the poor quadroon's eyes.

The daughter stood up, her eyes flashing.

"God made us, Maman," she said with a gentle, but stately smile.

"Ha!" said the mother, her keen glance darting through her tears, "Sin made *me*, yes."

"No," said 'Tite Poulette, "God made us. He made us just as we are; not more white, not more black."

"He made you, truly!" said Zalli. "You are so beautiful; I believe it well." She reached and drew the fair form to a kneeling posture. "My sweet, white daughter!"

Now the tears were in the girl's eyes. "And could I be whiter than I am?" she asked.

"Oh, no, no! 'Tite Poulette," cried the other; "but if we were only *real white!*—both of us; so that some gentleman might come to see me and say 'Madame John, I want your pretty little chick. She is so beautiful. I want to take her home. She is so good—I want her to be my wife.' Oh, my child, my child, to see that I would give my life—I would give my soul! Only you should take me along to be your servant. I walked behind two young men to-night; they were coming home from their office; presently they began to talk about you."

'Tite Poulette's eyes flashed fire.

"No, my child, they spoke only the best things. One laughed a little at times and kept saying 'Beware!' but the other — I prayed the Virgin to bless him, he spoke such kind and noble words. Such gentle pity; such a holy heart! 'May God defend her,' he said, *cherie;* he said, 'May God defend her, for I see no help for her.' The other one laughed and left him. He stopped in the door right across the street. Ah, my child, do you blush? Is that something to bring the rose to your cheek? Many fine gentlemen at the ball ask me often, 'How is your daughter, Madame John?'"

The daughter's face was thrown into the mother's lap, not so well satisfied, now, with God's handiwork. Ah, how she wept! Sob, sob, sob; gasps and sighs and stifled ejaculations, her small right hand clinched and beating on her mother's knee; and the mother weeping over her.

Kristian Koppig shut his window. Nothing but a generous heart and a Dutchman's phlegm could have done so at that moment. And even thou, Kristian Koppig! —— for the window closed very slowly.

He wrote to his mother, thus:

"In this wicked city, I see none so fair as the poor girl who lives opposite me, and who, alas! though so fair, is one of those whom the taint of caste has cursed. She lives a lonely, innocent life in the midst of corruption, like the lilies I find here in the marshes, and I have great pity for her. 'God defend her,' I said to-night to a fellow clerk, 'I see no help for her.' I know there is a natural, and I think proper, horror of mixed blood (excuse the mention, sweet mother), and I feel it, too ; and yet if she were in Holland to-day, not one of a hundred suitors would detect the hidden blemish.''

In such strain this young man wrote on trying to demonstrate the utter impossibility of his ever loving the lovable unfortunate, until the midnight tolling of the cathedral clock sent him to bed.

About the same hour Zalli and 'Tite Poulette were kissing good-night.

'' 'Tite Poulette, I want you to promise me one thing.''

'' Well, Maman?''

'' If any gentleman should ever love you and ask you to marry, — not knowing, you know, — promise me you will not tell him you are not white.''

'' It can never be,'' said 'Tite Poulette.

'' But if it should,'' said Madame John plead-ingly.

'' And break the law?'' asked 'Tite Poulette, im-patiently.

'' But the law is unjust,'' said the mother.

'' But it is the law!''

'' But you will not, dearie, will you?''

'' I would surely tell him!'' said the daughter.

When Zalli, for some cause, went next morning to the window, she started.

'' 'Tite Poulette!'' — she called softly without mov-ing. The daughter came. The young man, whose idea of propriety had actuated him to this display, was sitting in the dormer window, reading. Mother

and daughter bent a steady gaze at each other. It
meant in French, " If he saw us last night ! " —

" Ah ! dear," said the mother, her face beaming
with fun —

" What can it be, Maman?"

" He speaks — oh ! ha, ha ! — he speaks — such
miserable French ! "

It came to pass one morning at early dawn that Zalli
and 'Tite Poulette, going to mass, passed a café, just
as — who should be coming out but Monsieur, the
manager of the *Salle de Condé.* He had not yet gone
to bed. Monsieur was astonished. He had a Frenchman's eye for the beautiful, and certainly there the
beautiful was. He had heard of Madame John's
daughter, and had hoped once to see her, but did not ·
but could this be she?

They disappeared within the cathedral. A sudden
pang of piety moved him; he followed. 'Tite Poulette was already kneeling in the aisle. Zalli, still in
the vestibule, was just taking her hand from the font
of holy-water.

" Madame John," whispered the manager.

She courtesied.

" Madame John, that young lady — is she your
daughter?"

" She — she — is my daughter," said Zalli, with
somewhat of alarm in her face, which the manager
misinterpreted.

" I think not, Madame John." He shook his head,
smiling as one too wise to be fooled.

"Yes, Monsieur, she is my daughter."

"O no, Madame John, it is only make-believe, I think."

"I swear she is, Monsieur de la Rue."

"Is that possible?" pretending to waver, but convinced in his heart of hearts, by Zalli's alarm, that she was lying. "But how? Why does she not come to our ball-room with you?"

Zalli, trying to get away from him, shrugged and smiled. "Each to his taste, Monsieur; it pleases her not."

She was escaping, but he followed one step more. "I shall come to see you, Madame John."

She whirled and attacked him with her eyes. "Monsieur must not give himself the trouble!" she said, the eyes at the same time adding, "Dare to come!" She turned again, and knelt to her devotions. The manager dipped in the font, crossed himself, and departed.

Several weeks went by, and M. de la Rue had not accepted the fierce challenge of Madame John's eyes. One or two Sunday nights she had succeeded in avoiding him, though fulfilling her engagement in the *Salle;* but by and by pay-day, — a Saturday, — came round, and though the pay was ready, she was loath to go up to Monsieur's little office.

It was an afternoon in May. Madame John came to her own room, and, with a sigh, sank into a chair. Her eyes were wet.

"Did you go to his office, dear mother?" asked 'Tite Poulette.

"I could not," she answered, dropping her face in her hands.

"Maman, he has seen me at the window!"

"While I was gone?" cried the mother.

"He passed on the other side of the street. He looked up purposely, and saw me." The speaker's cheeks were burning red.

Zalli wrung her hands.

"It is nothing, mother; do not go near him."

"But the pay, my child."

"The pay matters not."

"But he will bring it here; he wants the chance."

That was the trouble, sure enough.

About this time Kristian Koppig lost his position in the German importing house where, he had fondly told his mother, he was indispensable.

"Summer was coming on," the senior said, "and you see our young men are almost idle. Yes, our engagement *was* for a year, but ah — we could not foresee" — etc., etc., "besides" (attempting a parting flattery), "your father is a rich gentleman, and you can afford to take the summer easy. If we can ever be of any service to you," etc., etc.

So the young Dutchman spent the afternoons at his dormer window reading and glancing down at the little casement opposite, where a small, rude shelf had lately been put out, holding a row of cigar-boxes with wretched little botanical specimens in them trying to die. 'Tite Poulette was their gardener; and it was odd to see, — dry weather or wet, — how many waterings per day those plants could take. She never looked

up from her task; but I know she performed it with
that unacknowledged pleasure which all girls love and
deny, that of being looked upon by noble eyes.

On this peculiar Saturday afternoon in May, Kristian
Koppig had been witness of the distressful scene over
the way. It occurred to 'Tite Poulette that such might
be the case, and she stepped to the casement to shut
it. As she did so, the marvellous delicacy of Kristian
Koppig moved him to draw in one of his shutters.
Both young heads came out at one moment, while at
the same instant —

"Rap, rap, rap, rap, rap!" clanked the knocker on
the wicket. The black eyes of the maiden and the
blue over the way, from looking into each other for
the first time in life, glanced down to the arched doorway upon Monsieur the manager. Then the black
eyes disappeared within, and Kristian Koppig thought
again, and re-opening his shutter, stood up at the window prepared to become a bold spectator of what
might follow.

But for a moment nothing followed.

"Trouble over there," thought the rosy Dutchman,
and waited. The manager waited too, rubbing his hat
and brushing his clothes with the tips of his kidded
fingers.

"They do not wish to see him," slowly concluded
the spectator.

"Rap, rap, rap, rap, rap!" quoth the knocker, and
M. de la Rue looked up around at the windows opposite and noticed the handsome young Dutchman
looking at him.

"Dutch!" said the manager softly, between his teeth.

"He is staring at me," said Kristian Koppig to himself;—"but then I am staring at him, which accounts for it."

A long pause, and then another long rapping.

"They want him to go away," thought Koppig.

"Knock hard!" suggested a street youngster, standing by.

"Rap, rap"— The manager had no sooner recommenced than several neighbors looked out of doors and windows.

"Very bad," thought our Dutchman; "somebody should make him go off. I wonder what they will do."

The manager stepped into the street, looked up at the closed window, returned to the knocker, and stood with it in his hand.

"They are all gone out, Monsieur," said the street-youngster.

"You lie!" said the cynosure of neighboring eyes.

"Ah!" thought Kristian Koppig; "I will go down and ask him "— Here his thoughts lost outline; he was only convinced that he had somewhat to say to him, and turned to go down stairs. In going he became a little vexed with himself because he could not help hurrying. He noticed, too, that his arm holding the stair-rail trembled in a silly way, whereas he was perfectly calm. Precisely as he reached the street-door the manager raised the knocker; but the latch clicked and the wicket was drawn slightly ajar.

Inside could just be descried Madame John. The manager bowed, smiled, talked, talked on, held money in his hand, bowed, smiled, talked on, flourished the money, smiled, bowed, talked on and plainly persisted in some intention to which Madame John was steadfastly opposed.

The window above, too, — it was Kristian Koppig who noticed that, — opened a wee bit, like the shell of a terrapin. Presently the manager lifted his foot and put forward an arm, as though he would enter the gate by pushing, but as quick as gunpowder it clapped — in his face!

You could hear the fleeing feet of Zalli pounding up the staircase.

As the panting mother re-entered her room, "See, Maman," said 'Tite Poulette, peeping at the window, "the young gentleman from over the way has crossed!"

"Holy Mary bless him!" said the mother.

"I will go over," thought Kristian Koppig, "and ask him kindly if he is not making a mistake."

"What are they doing, dear?" asked the mother, with clasped hands.

"They are talking; the young man is tranquil, but 'Sieur de la Rue is very angry," whispered the daughter; and just then — pang! came a sharp, keen sound rattling up the walls on either side of the narrow way, and "Aha!" and laughter and clapping of female hands from two or three windows.

"Oh! what a slap!" cried the girl, half in fright, half in glee, jerking herself back from the casement

simultaneously with the report. But the " ahas " and
laughter, and clapping of feminine hands, which still
continued, came from another cause. 'Tite Poulette's
rapid action had struck the slender cord that held up
an end of her hanging garden, and the whole rank of
cigar-boxes slid from their place, turned gracefully
over as they shot through the air, and emptied them-
themselves plump upon the head of the slapped manager. Breathless, dirty, pale as whitewash, he gasped a
threat to be heard from again, and, getting round the
corner as quick as he could walk, left Kristian Koppig,
standing motionless, the most astonished man in that
street.

"Kristian Koppig, Kristian Koppig," said Great-
heart to himself, slowly dragging up-stairs, "what a
mischief you have done. One poor woman certainly
to be robbed of her bitter wages, and another — so
lovely! — put to the burning shame of being the subject of a street brawl! What will this silly neighborhood say? 'Has the gentleman a heart as well as a
hand?' 'Is it jealousy?' " There he paused, afraid
himself to answer the supposed query; and then —
"Oh! Kristian Koppig, you have been such a dunce!"
"And I cannot apologize to them. Who in this street
would carry my note, and not wink and grin over it
with low surmises? I cannot even make restitution.
Money? They would not dare receive it. Oh! Kristian Koppig, why *did* you not mind your own business?
Is she any thing to you? Do you love her? *Of course
not!* Oh! — such a dunce!"

The reader will eagerly admit that however faulty

this young man's course of reasoning, his conclusion was correct. For mark what he did.

He went to his room, which was already growing dark, shut his window, lighted his big Dutch lamp, and sat down to write. "Something *must* be done," said he aloud, taking up his pen; "I will be calm and cool; I will be distant and brief; but — I shall have to be kind or I may offend. Ah! I shall have to write in French; I forgot that; I write it so poorly, dunce that I am, when all my brothers and sisters speak it so well." He got out his French dictionary. Two hours slipped by. He made a new pen, washed and refilled his inkstand, mended his "abominable!" chair, and after two hours more made another attempt, and another failure. "My head aches," said he, and lay down on his couch, the better to frame his phrases.

He was awakened by the Sabbath sunlight. The bells of the Cathedral and the Ursulines' chapel were ringing for high mass, and a mocking-bird, perching on a chimney-top above Madame John's rooms, was carolling, whistling, mewing, chirping, screaming, and trilling with the ecstasy of a whole May in his throat. "Oh! sleepy Kristian Koppig," was the young man's first thought, " — such a dunce!"

Madame John and daughter did not go to mass. The morning wore away, and their casement remained closed. "They are offended," said Kristian Koppig, leaving the house, and wandering up to the little Protestant affair known as Christ Church.

"No, possibly they are not," he said, returning and finding the shutters thrown back.

By a sad accident, which mortified him extremely, he happened to see, late in the afternoon, — hardly conscious that he was looking across the street, — that Madame John was — dressing. Could it be that she was going to the *Salle de Condé?* He rushed to his table, and began to write.

He had guessed aright. The wages were too precious to be lost. The manager had written her a note. He begged to assure her that he was a gentleman of the clearest cut. If he had made a mistake the previous afternoon, he was glad no unfortunate result had followed except his having been assaulted by a ruffian ; that the *Danse du Shawl* was promised in his advertisement, and he hoped Madame John (whose wages were in hand waiting for her) would not fail to assist as usual. Lastly, and delicately put, he expressed his conviction that Mademoiselle was wise and discreet in declining to entertain gentlemen at her home.

So, against much beseeching on the part of 'Tite Poulette, Madame John was going to the ball-room. "Maybe I can discover what 'Sieur de la Rue is planning against Monsieur over the way," she said, knowing certainly the slap would not be forgiven; and the daughter, though tremblingly, at once withdrew her objections.

The heavy young Dutchman, now thoroughly electrified, was writing like mad. He wrote and tore up, wrote and tore up, lighted his lamp, started again, and

at last signed his name. A letter by a Dutchman in
French!— what can be made of it in English? We
will see:

"MADAME AND MADEMOISELLE:

"A stranger, seeking not to be acquainted, but seeing and
admiring all days the goodness and high honor, begs to be pardoned of them for the mistakes, alas! of yesterday, and to
make reparation and satisfaction in destroying the ornaments
of the window, as well as the loss of compensation from Monsieur the manager, with the enclosed bill of the *Banque de la
Louisiane* for fifty dollars ($50). And, hoping they will seeing
what he is meaning, remains, respectfully,

"KRISTIAN KOPPIG.

"P.S.— Madame must not go to the ball."

He must bear the missive himself. He must speak
in French. What should the words be? A moment
of study— he has it, and is off down the long three-
story stairway. At the same moment Madame John
stepped from the wicket, and glided off to the *Salle
de Condé*, a trifle late.

"I shall see Madame John, of course," thought
the young man, crushing a hope, and rattled the
knocker. 'Tite Poulette sprang up from praying for
her mother's safety. "What has she forgotten?"
she asked herself, and hastened down. The wicket
opened. The two innocents were stunned.

"Aw— aw"— said the pretty Dutchman, "aw,"
— blurted out something in virgin Dutch, . . . handed her the letter, and hurried down street.

"Alas! what have I done?" said the poor girl,
bending over her candle, and bursting into tears that

fell on the unopened letter. "And what shall I do? It may be wrong to open it — and worse not to." Like her sex, she took the benefit of the doubt, and intensified her perplexity and misery by reading and misconstruing the all but unintelligible contents. What then? Not only sobs and sighs, but moaning and beating of little fists together, and outcries of soul-felt agony stifled against the bedside, and temples pressed into knitted palms, because of one who "sought *not to be* acquainted," but offered money — money! — in pity to a poor — shame on her for saying that! — a poor *nigresse*.

And now our self-confessed dolt turned back from a half-hour's walk, concluding there might be an answer to his note. "Surely Madame John will appear this time." He knocked. The shutter stirred above, and something white came fluttering wildly down like a shot dove. It was his own letter containing the fifty-dollar bill. He bounded to the wicket, and softly but eagerly knocked again.

"Go away," said a trembling voice from above.

"Madame John?" said he; but the window closed, and he heard a step, the same step on the stair. Step, step, every step one step deeper into his heart. 'Tite Poulette came to the closed door.

"What will you?" said the voice within.

"I — I — don't wish to see you. I wish to see Madame John."

"I must pray Monsieur to go away. My mother is at the *Salle de Condé*."

"At the ball!" Kristian Koppig strayed off, re-

peating the words for want of definite thought. All at
once it occurred to him that at the ball he could make
Madame John's acquaintance with impunity. "Was
it courting sin to go?" By no means; he should,
most likely, save a woman from trouble, and help the
poor in their distress.

Behold Kristian Koppig standing on the floor of the
Salle de Condé. A large hall, a blaze of lamps, a be-
wildering flutter of fans and floating robes, strains
of music, columns of gay promenaders, a long row of
turbaned mothers lining either wall, gentlemen of the
portlier sort filling the recesses of the windows, whirling waltzers gliding here and there — smiles and grace,
smiles and grace; all fair, orderly, elegant, bewitch-
ing. A young Creole's laugh mayhap a little loud,
and — truly there were many sword-canes. But
neither grace nor foulness satisfied the eye of the
zealous young Dutchman.

Suddenly a muffled woman passed him, leaning on a
gentleman's arm. It looked like — it must be, Madame John. Speak quick, Kristian Koppig; do not
stop to notice the man!

"Madame John" — bowing — "I am your neighbor, Kristian Koppig."

Madame John bows low, and smiles — a ball-room
smile, but is frightened, and her escort, — the manager, — drops her hand and slips away.

"Ah! Monsieur," she whispers excitedly, "you
will be killed if you stay here a moment. Are you
armed? No. Take this." She tried to slip a dirk
into his hands, but he would not have it.

"Oh, my dear young man, go! Go quickly!" she plead, glancing furtively down the hall.

"I wish you not to dance," said the young man.

"I have danced already; I am going home. Come; be quick! we will go together." She thrust her arm through his, and they hastened into the street. When a square had been passed there came a sound of men running behind them.

"Run, Monsieur, run!" she cried, trying to drag him; but Monsieur Dutchman would not.

"*Run*, Monsieur! Oh, my God! it is 'Sieur" —

"*That* for yesterday!" cried the manager, striking fiercely with his cane. Kristian Koppig's fist rolled him in the dirt.

"*That* for 'Tite Poulette!" cried another man dealing the Dutchman a terrible blow from behind.

"And *that* for me!" hissed a third, thrusting at him with something bright.

"*That* for yesterday!" screamed the manager, bounding like a tiger; "That!" "THAT!" "Ha!"

Then Kristian Koppig knew that he was stabbed.

"That!" and "That!" and "That!" and the poor Dutchman struck wildly here and there, grasped the air, shut his eyes, staggered, reeled, fell, rose half up, fell again for good, and they were kicking him and jumping on him. All at once they scampered. Zalli had found the night-watch.

"Buz-z-z-z!" went a rattle. "Buz-z-z-z!" went another.

"Pick him up."

"Is he alive?"

"Can't tell; hold him steady; lead the way, misses."

"He's bleeding all over my breeches."

"This way — here — around this corner."

"This way now — only two squares more."

"Here we are."

"Rap-rap-rap!" on the old brass knocker. Curses on the narrow wicket, more on the dark archway, more still on the twisting stairs.

Up at last and into the room.

"Easy, easy, push this under his head! never mind his boots!"

So he lies — on 'Tite Poulette's own bed.

The watch are gone. They pause under the corner lamp to count profits; — a single bill — *Banque de la Louisiane*, fifty dollars. Providence is kind — tolerably so. Break it at the "Guillaume Tell." "But did you ever hear any one scream like that girl did?"

And there lies the young Dutch neighbor. His money will not flutter back to him this time; nor will any voice behind a gate "beg Monsieur to go away." O, Woman! — that knows no enemy so terrible as man! Come nigh, poor Woman, you have nothing to fear. Lay your strange, electric touch upon the chilly flesh; it strikes no eager mischief along the fainting veins. Look your sweet looks upon the grimy face, and tenderly lay back the locks from the congested brows; no wicked misinterpretation lurks to bite your kindness. Be motherly, be sisterly, fear nought. Go, watch him by night; you may sleep at his feet and he will not stir. Yet he lives, and shall live — may live to forget yo , knows? But for all that, be gentle

and watchful; be womanlike, we ask no more; and
God reward you!

Even while it was taking all the two women's
strength to hold the door against Death, the sick man
himself laid a grief upon them.

"Mother," he said to Madame John, quite a master
of French in his delirium, "dear mother, fear not;
trust your boy; fear nothing. I will not marry 'Tite
Poulette; I cannot. She is fair, dear mother, but ah!
she is not — don't you know, mother? don't you
know? The race! the race! Don't you know that
she is jet black. Isn't it?"

The poor nurse nodded "Yes," and gave a sleeping
draught; but before the patient quite slept he started
once and stared.

"Take her away," — waving his hand — "take your
beauty away. She is jet white. Who could take a
jet white wife? O, no, no, no, no!"

Next morning his brain was right.

"Madame," he weakly whispered, "I was delirious
last night?"

Zalli shrugged. "Only a very, very, wee, wee trifle
of a bit."

"And did I say something wrong or — foolish?"

"O, no, no," she replied; "you only clasped your
hands, so, and prayed, prayed all the time to the dear
Virgin."

"To the virgin?" asked the Dutchman, smiling incredulously.

"And St. Joseph — yes, indeed," she insisted;
"you may strike me dead."

And so, for politeness' sake, he tried to credit the invention, but grew suspicious instead.

Hard was the battle against death. Nurses are sometimes amazons, and such were these. Through the long, enervating summer, the contest lasted; but when at last the cool airs of October came stealing in at the bedside like long-banished little children, Kristian Koppig rose upon his elbow and smiled them a welcome.

The physician, blessed man, was kind beyond measure; but said some inexplicable things, which Zalli tried in vain to make him speak in an undertone. "If I knew Monsieur John?" he said, "certainly! Why, we were chums at school. And he left you so much as that, Madame John? Ah! my old friend John, always noble! And you had it all in that naughty bank? Ah, well, Madame John, it matters little. No, I shall not tell 'Tite Poulette. Adieu."

And another time:—"If I will let you tell me something? With pleasure, Madame John. No, and not tell anybody, Madame John. No, Madame, not even 'Tite Poulette. What?"—a long whistle—"is that pos-si-ble?—and Monsieur John knew it?—encouraged it?—eh, well, eh, well!—But—can I believe you, Madame John? Oh! you have Monsieur John's sworn statement. Ah! very good, truly, but—you *say* you have it; but where is it? Ah! to-morrow!" a sceptical shrug. "Pardon me, Madame John, I think perhaps, *perhaps* you are telling the truth.

"If I think you did right? Certainly! What na-

ture keeps back, accident sometimes gives, Madame
John; either is God's will. Don't cry. 'Stealing
from the dead?' No! It was giving, yes! They
are thanking you in heaven, Madame John."

Kristian Koppig, lying awake, but motionless and
with closed eyes, hears in part, and, fancying he under-
stands, rejoices with silent intensity. When the doctor is gone he calls Zalli.

"I give you a great deal of trouble, eh, Madame
John?"

"No, no; you are no trouble at all. Had you the
yellow fever — ah! then!"

She rolled her eyes to signify the superlative character of the tribulations attending yellow fever.

"I had a lady and gentleman once — a Spanish lady
and gentleman, just off the ship; both sick at once
with the fever — delirious — could not tell their names.
Nobody to help me but sometimes Monsieur John! I
never had such a time, — never before, never since, —
as that time. Four days and nights this head touched
not a pillow."

"And they died!" said Kristian Koppig.

"The third night the gentleman went. Poor Señor!
'Sieur John, — he did not know the harm, — gave him
some coffee and toast! The fourth night it rained and
turned cool, and just before day the poor lady " —

"Died!" said Koppig.

Zalli dropped her arms listlessly into her lap and her
eyes ran brimful.

"And left an infant!" said the Dutchman, ready to
shout with exultation.

"Ah! no, Monsieur," said Zalli.

The invalid's heart sank like a stone.

"Madame John," — his voice was all in a tremor, — "tell me the truth. Is 'Tite Poulette your own child?"

"Ah-h-h, ha! ha! what foolishness! Of course she is my child!" And Madame gave vent to a true Frenchwoman's laugh.

It was too much for the sick man. In the pitiful weakness of his shattered nerves he turned his face into his pillow and wept like a child. Zalli passed into the next room to hide her emotion.

"Maman, dear Maman," said 'Tite Poulette, who had overheard nothing, but only saw the tears.

"Ah! my child, my child, my task — my task is too great — too great for me. Let me go now — another time. Go and watch at his bedside."

"But, Maman," — for 'Tite Poulette was frightened, — "he needs no care now."

"Nay, but go, my child; I wish to be alone."

The maiden stole in with averted eyes and tiptoed to the window — *that window*. The patient, already a man again, gazed at her till she could feel the gaze. He turned his eyes from her a moment to gather resolution. And now, stout heart, farewell; a word or two of friendly parting — nothing more.

"'Tite Poulette."

The slender figure at the window turned and came to the bedside.

"I believe I owe my life to you," he said.

She looked down meekly, the color rising in her cheek

"I must arrange to be moved across the street to-morrow, on a litter."

She did not stir or speak.

"And I must now thank you, sweet nurse, for your care. Sweet nurse! Sweet nurse!"

She shook her head in protestation.

"Heaven bless you, 'Tite Poulette!"

Her face sank lower.

"God has made you very beautiful, 'Tite Poulette!"

She stirred not. He reached, and gently took her little hand, and as he drew her one step nearer, a tear fell from her long lashes. From the next room, Zalli, with a face of agonized suspense, gazed upon the pair, undiscovered. The young man lifted the hand to lay it upon his lips, when, with a mild, firm force, it was drawn away, yet still rested in his own upon the bed-side, like some weak thing snared, that could only not get free.

"Thou wilt not have my love, 'Tite Poulette?"

No answer.

"Thou wilt not, beautiful?"

"Cannot!" was all that she could utter, and upon their clasped hands the tears ran down.

"Thou wrong'st me, 'Tite Poulette. Thou dost not trust me; thou fearest the kiss may loosen the hands. But I tell thee nay. I have struggled hard, even to this hour, against Love, but I yield me now; I yield; I am his unconditioned prisoner forever. God forbid that I ask aught but that you will be my wife."

Still the maiden moved not, looked not up, only rained down tears.

" Shall it not be, 'Tite Poulette?" He tried in vain to draw her.

" 'Tite Poulette?" So tenderly he called! And then she spoke.

" It is against the law."

" It is not!" cried Zalli, seizing her round the waist and dragging her forward. "Take her! she is thine. I have robbed God long enough. Here are the sworn papers — here! Take her; she is as white as snow — so! Take her, kiss her; Mary be praised! I never had a child — she is the Spaniard's daughter!"

'Sieur George

'SIEUR GEORGE.

In the heart of New Orleans stands a large four-story brick building, that has so stood for about three-quarters of a century. Its rooms are rented to a class of persons occupying them simply for lack of activity to find better and cheaper quarters elsewhere. With its gray stucco peeling off in broad patches, it has a solemn look of gentility in rags, and stands, or, as it were, hangs, about the corner of two ancient streets, like a faded fop who pretends to be looking for employment.

Under its main archway is a dingy apothecary-shop. On one street is the bazaar of a *modiste en robes et chapeaux* and other humble shops; on the other, the immense batten doors with gratings over the lintels, barred and bolted with masses of cobwebbed iron, like the door of a donjon, are overhung by a creaking sign (left by the sheriff), on which is faintly discernible the mention of wines and liquors. A peep through one of the shops reveals a square court within, hung with many lines of wet clothes, its sides hugged by rotten staircases that seem vainly trying to clamber out of the rubbish.

The neighborhood is one long since given up to fifth-rate shops, whose masters and mistresses display such enticing mottoes as "*Au gagne petit!*" Innumerable children swarm about, and, by some charm of the place, are not run over, but obstruct the sidewalks playing their clamorous games

The building is a thing of many windows, where passably good-looking women appear and disappear, clad in cotton gowns, watering little outside shelves of flowers and cacti, or hanging canaries' cages. Their husbands are keepers in wine-warehouses, rent-collectors for the agents of old Frenchmen who have been laid up to dry in Paris, custom-house supernumeraries and court-clerks' deputies (for your second-rate Creole is a great seeker for little offices). A decaying cornice hangs over, dropping bits of mortar on passers below, like a boy at a boarding-house.

The landlord is one Kookoo, an ancient Creole of doubtful purity of blood, who in his landlordly old age takes all suggestions of repairs as personal insults. He was but a stripling when his father left him this inheritance, and has grown old and wrinkled and brown, a sort of periodically animate mummy, in the business. He smokes cascarilla, wears velveteen, and is as punctual as an executioner.

To Kookoo's venerable property a certain old man used for many years to come every evening, stumbling through the groups of prattling children who frolicked about in the early moonlight — whose name no one knew, but whom all the neighbors designated by the title of 'Sieur George. It was his wont to be seen taking a straight—too straight—course toward his home, never careening to right or left, but now forcing himself slowly forward, as though there were a high gale in front, and now scudding briskly ahead at a ridiculous little dog-trot, as if there were a tornado behind. He would go up the main staircase very carefully, sometimes stopping half-way up for thirty or forty minutes' doze, but getting to the landing eventually, and tramping into his room in the second story, with no little elation to find it still there. Were it not for these slight symptoms of potations, he was such a one as you would pick out of a thousand for a miser. A year or two ago he suddenly disappeared.

A great many years ago, when the old house was still new, a young man with no baggage save a small hair-trunk, came and took the room I have mentioned and another adjoining. He supposed he might stay fifty days—and he staid fifty years and over. This was a very fashionable neighborhood, and he kept the rooms on that account month after month.

But when he had been here about a year something happened to him, so it was rumored, that greatly changed the tenor of his life; and from that time on there began to appear in him and to accumulate upon each other in a manner which became the profound study of Kookoo, the symptoms of a decay, whose cause baffled the landlord's limited powers of conjecture for well-nigh half a century. Hints of a duel, of a reason warped, of disinheritance, and many other unauthorized rumors, fluttered up and floated off, while he became recluse, and, some say, began incidentally to betray the unmanly habit which we have already noticed. His neighbors would have continued neighborly had he allowed them, but he never let himself be understood, and *les Américains* are very droll anyhow ; so, as they could do nothing else, they cut him.

So exclusive he became that (though it may have been for economy) he never admitted even a housemaid, but kept his apartments himself. Only the merry serenaders, who in those times used to sing under the balconies, would now and then give him a crumb of their feast for pure fun's sake ; and after a while, because they could not find out his full name, called him, at hazard, George — but always prefixing Monsieur. Afterward, when he began to be careless in his dress, and the fashion of serenading had passed away, the commoner people dared to shorten the title to " 'Sieur George."

Many seasons came and went. The city changed like a growing boy ; gentility and fashion went uptown, but 'Sieur George still retained his rooms. Every one knew him slightly, and bowed, but no one seemed to know him well, unless it were a brace or so of those convivial fellows in regulation-blue at little Fort St. Charles. He often came home late, with one of these on either arm, all singing different tunes and stopping at every twenty steps to tell secrets. But by and by the fort was demolished, church and goverment property melted down under the warm demand for building-lots, the city spread like a ringworm, — and one day 'Sieur George steps out of the old house in full regimentals !

The Creole neighbors rush bareheaded into the middle of the street, as though there were an earthquake or a chimney on fire. What to do or say or think they do not know; they are at their wits' ends, therefore well-nigh happy. However, there is a German blacksmith's shop near by, and they watch to see what *Jacob* will do. Jacob steps into the street with every eye upon him; he approaches Monsieur — he addresses to him a few remarks — they shake hands — they engage in some conversation — Monsieur places his hand on his sword! — now Monsieur passes.

The populace crowd around the blacksmith, children clap their hands softly and jump up and down on tiptoes of expectation — 'Sieur George is going to the war in Mexico!

"Ah!" says a little girl in the throng, "'Sieur George's two rooms will be empty; I find that very droll."

The landlord, — this same Kookoo, — is in the group. He hurls himself into the house and up the stairs. "Fifteen years pass since he have been in those room!" He arrives at the door — it is shut — "It is lock!"

In short, further investigation revealed that a youngish lady in black, who had been seen by several neighbors to enter the house, but had not, of course, been suspected of such remarkable intentions, had, in company with a middle-aged slave-woman, taken these two rooms, and now, at the slightly-opened door, proffered a month's rent in advance. What could a landlord do but smile? Yet there was a pretext left,

" the rooms must need repairs?" — " No, sir; he
could look in and see." Joy! he looked in. All was
neatness. The floor unbroken, the walls cracked but
a little, and the cracks closed with new plaster, no
doubt by the jealous hand of 'Sieur George himself
Kookoo's eyes swept sharply round the two apartments. The furniture was all there. Moreover, there
was Monsieur's little hair-trunk. He should not soon
forget that trunk. One day, fifteen years or more
before, he had taken hold of that trunk to assist Monsieur to arrange his apartment, and Monsieur had
drawn his fist back and cried to him to "drop it!"
Mais! there it was, looking very suspicious in Kookoo's eyes, and the lady's domestic, as tidy as a
yellow-bird, went and sat on it. Could that trunk
contain treasure? It might, for Madame wanted to
shut the door, and, in fact, did so.

The lady was quite handsome — had been more so,
but was still young — spoke the beautiful language,
and kept, in the inner room, her discreet and taciturn
mulattress, a tall, straight woman, with a fierce eye,
but called by the young Creoles of the neighborhood
" confound' good lookin'."

Among les Américaines, where the new neighbor
always expects to be called upon by the older residents, this lady might have made friends in spite of
being as reserved as 'Sieur George; but the reverse
being the Creole custom, and she being well pleased to
keep her own company, chose mystery rather than
society.

The poor landlord was sorely troubled; it must not

that any thing *de trop* take place in his house. He watched the two rooms narrowly, but without result, save to find that Madame plied her needle for pay, spent her money for little else besides harpstrings. and took good care of the little trunk of Monsieur. This espionage was a good turn to the mistress and maid, for when Kookoo announced that all was proper, no more was said by outsiders. Their landlord never got but one question answered by the middle-aged maid:

"Madame, he feared, was a litt' bit embarrass' *pour* money, eh?"

"*Non;* Mademoiselle [Mademoiselle, you notice!] had some property, but did not want to eat it up."

Sometimes lady-friends came, in very elegant private carriages, to see her, and one or two seemed to beg her — but in vain — to go away with them; but these gradually dropped off, until lady and servant were alone in the world. And so years, and the Mexican war, went by.

The volunteers came home; peace reigned, and the city went on spreading up and down the land; but 'Sieur George did not return. It overran the country like cocoa-grass. Fields, roads, woodlands, that were once 'Sieur George's places of retreat from mankind, were covered all over with little one-story houses in the "Old Third," and fine residences and gardens up in "Lafayette." Streets went slicing like a butcher's knife, through old colonial estates, whose first masters never dreamed of the city reaching them, — and 'Sieur George was still away The four-story brick got o'd and ugly, and the surroundings dim and dreamy. Theatres, processions, dry-goods stores, government establishments, banks, hotels, and all spirit of enterprise were gone to Canal Street and beyond, and the very beggars were gone with them. The little trunk got very old and bald, and still its owner lingered; still the lady, somewhat the worse for lapse of time, looked from the balcony-window in the brief southern twilights, and the maid every morning shook a worn rug or two over the dangerous-looking railing; and yet neither had made friends or enemies.

The two rooms, from having been stingily kept at first, were needing repairs half the time, and the occupants were often moving, now into one, now back into the other; yet the hair-trunk was seen only by glimpses, the landlord, to his infinite chagrin, always being a little too late in offering his services, the women, whether it was light or heavy, having already moved it. He thought it significant.

Late one day of a most bitter winter, — that season when, to the ecstatic amazement of a whole city-full of children, snow covered the streets ankle-deep, — there came a soft tap on the corridor-door of this pair of rooms. The lady opened it, and beheld a tall, lank, iron-gray man, a total stranger, standing behind — Monsieur George! Both men were weather-beaten, scarred, and tattered. Across 'Sieur George's crown, leaving a long, bare streak through his white hair, was the souvenir of a Mexican sabre.

The landlord had accompanied them to the door: it was a magnificent opportunity. Mademoiselle asked them all in, and tried to furnish a seat to each; but failing, 'Sieur George went straight across the room and *sat on the hair-trunk*. The action was so conspicuous, the landlord laid it up in his penetrative mind.

'Sieur George was quiet, or, as it appeared, quieted. The mulattress stood near him, and to her he addressed, in an undertone, most of the little he said, leaving Mademoiselle to his companion. The stranger was a warm talker, and seemed to please the lady from the first; but if he pleased, nothing else did. Kookoo, intensely curious, sought some pretext for staying, but found none. They were, altogether, an uncongenial company. The lady seemed to think Kookoo had no business there; 'Sieur George seemed to think the same concerning his companion; and the few words between Mademoiselle and 'Sieur George were cool enough. The maid appeared nearly satisfied, but could not avoid casting an anxious eye at times upon her mistress. Naturally the visit was short.

The next day but one the two gentlemen came again in better attire. 'Sieur George evidently disliked his companion, yet would not rid himself of him. The stranger was a gesticulating, stagy fellow, much Monsieur's junior, an incessant talker in Creole-French, always excited on small matters and unable to appreciate a great one. Once, as they were leaving, Kookoo, — accidents will happen, — was under the stairs. As they began to descend the tall man was speaking: " — better to bury it," — the startled landlord heard him say, and held his breath, thinking of the trunk; but no more was uttered.

A week later they came again.

A week later they came again.

A week later they came yet again!

The landlord's eyes began to open. There must be a courtship in progress. It was very plain now why 'Sieur George had wished not to be accompanied by the tall gentleman; but since his visits had become regular and frequent, it was equally plain why he did not get rid of him; — because it would not look well to be going and coming too often alone. Maybe it was only this tender passion that the tall man had thought "better to bury." Lately there often came sounds of gay conversation from the first of the two rooms, which had been turned into a parlor; and as, week after week, the friends came down-stairs, the tall man was always in high spirits and anxious to embrace 'Sieur George, who, — "sly dog," thought the landlord, — would try to look grave, and only smiled in an embarrassed way. "Ah! Monsieur, you tink to be varry conning; *mais* you not so conning as Kookoo, no;" and the inquisitive little man would shake his head and smile, and shake his head again, as a man has a perfect right to do under the conviction that he has been for twenty years baffled by a riddle and is learning to read it at last; he had guessed what was in 'Sieur George's head, he would by and by guess what was in the trunk.

A few months passed quickly away, and it became apparent to every eye in or about the ancient mansion that the landlord's guess was not so bad; in fact, that Mademoiselle was to be married.

On a certain rainy spring afternoon, a single hired hack drove up to the main entrance of the old house, and after some little bustle and the gathering of a crowd of damp children about the big doorway, 'Sieur George, muffled in a newly-repaired overcoat, jumped out and went up-stairs. A moment later he re-appeared, leading Mademoiselle, wreathed and veiled, down the stairway. Very fair was Mademoiselle still. Her beauty was mature, — fully ripe, — maybe a little too much so, but only a little ; and as she came down with the ravishing odor of bridal flowers floating about her, she seemed the garlanded victim of a pagan sacrifice. The mulattress in holiday gear followed behind.

The landlord owed a duty to the community. He arrested the maid on the last step: "Your mistress, she goin' *pour marier* 'Sieur George? It make me glad, glad, glad!"

"Marry 'Sieur George? Non, Monsieur."

"Non? Not marrie 'Sieur George? *Mais comment?*"

"She's going to marry the tall gentleman."

"*Diable!* ze long gentyman!" —With his hands upon his forehead, he watched the carriage trundle away. It passed out of sight through the rain ; he turned to enter the house, and all at once tottered under the weight of a tremendous thought — they had left the trunk! He hurled himself up-stairs as he had done seven years before, but again— "Ah, bah!!" —the door was locked, and not a picayune of rent due.

Late that night a small square man, in a wet over-

coat, fumbled his way into the damp entrance of the
house, stumbled up the cracking stairs, unlocked, after
many languid efforts, the door of the two rooms, and
falling over the hair-trunk, slept until the morning
sunbeams climbed over the balcony and in at the window, and shone full on the back of his head. Old
Kookoo, passing the door just then, was surprised to
find it slightly ajar — pushed it open silently, and saw,
within, 'Sieur George in the act of rising from his
knees beside the mysterious trunk! He had come
back to be once more the tenant of the two rooms.

'Sieur George, for the second time, was a changed
man — changed from bad to worse; from being retired
and reticent, he had come, by reason of advancing
years, or mayhap that which had left the terrible scar
on his face, to be garrulous. When, once in a while,
employment sought him (for he never sought employment), whatever remuneration he received went its
way for something that left him dingy and threadbare.
He now made a lively acquaintance with his landlord,
as, indeed, with every soul in the neighborhood, and
told all his adventures in Mexican prisons and Cuban
cities; including full details of the hardships and per-
ils experienced jointly with the "long gentleman"
who had married Mademoiselle, and who was no Mexican or Cuban, but a genuine Louisianian.

"It was he that fancied me," he said, "not I him;
but once he had fallen in love with me I hadn't the
force to cast him off. How Madame ever should have
liked him was one of those woman's freaks that a man
mustn't expect to understand. He was no more fit

for her than rags are fit for a queen; and I could have choked his head off the night he hugged me round the neck and told me what a suicide she had committed. But other fine women are committing that same folly every day, only they don't wait until they're thirty-four or five to do it. — ' Why don't I like him?' Well, for one reason, he's a drunkard!'" Here Kookoo, whose imperfect knowledge of English prevented his intelligent reception of the story, would laugh as if the joke came in just at this point.

However, with all Monsieur's prattle, he never dropped a word about the man he had been before he went away; and the great hair-trunk puzzle was still the same puzzle, growing greater every day.

Thus the two rooms had been the scene of some events quite queer, if not really strange; but the queerest that ever they presented, I guess, was 'Sieur George coming in there one day, crying like a little child, and bearing in his arms an infant — a girl — the lovely offspring of the drunkard whom he so detested, and poor, robbed, spirit-broken and now dead Madame. He took good care of the orphan, for orphan she was very soon. The long gentleman was pulled out of the Old Basin one morning, and 'Sieur George identified the body at the Trémé station. He never hired a nurse — the father had sold the lady's maid quite out of sight; so he brought her through all the little ills and around all the sharp corners of baby-life and child-hood, without a human hand to help him, until one evening, having persistently shut his eyes to it for weeks and months, like one trying to sleep in the sunshine, he awoke to the realization that she was a woman. It was a smoky one in November, the first cool day of autumn. The sunset was dimmed by the smoke of burning prairies, the air was full of the ashes of grass and reeds, ragged urchins were lugging home sticks of cordwood, and when a bit of coal fell from a cart in front of Kookoo's old house, a child was boxed half across the street and robbed of the booty by a *blanchisseuse de fin* from over the way.

The old man came home quite steady. He mounted the stairs smartly without stopping to rest, went with a step unusually light and quiet to his chamber and sat by the window opening upon the rusty balcony.

It was a small room, sadly changed from what it had been in old times; but then so was 'Sieur George. Close and dark it was, the walls stained with dampness and the ceiling full of bald places that showed the lathing. The furniture was cheap and meagre, including conspicuously the small, curious-looking hair-trunk. The floor was of wide slabs fastened down with spikes, and sloping up and down in one or two broad undulations, as if they had drifted far enough down the current of time to feel the tide-swell.

However, the floor was clean, the bed well made, the cypress table in place, and the musty smell of the walls partly neutralized by a geranium on the window-sill.

He so coming in and sitting down, an unseen person called from the room adjoining (of which, also, he was still the rentee), to know if he were he, and being answered in the affirmative, said, "Papa George, guess who was here to-day?"

"Kookoo, for the rent?"

"Yes, but he will not come back."

"No? why not?"

"Because you will not pay him."

"No? and why not?"

"Because I have paid him."

"Impossible! where did you get the money?'

"Cannot guess? — Mother Nativity."

"What, not for embroidery?"

"No? and why not? *Mais oui!*" — saying which, and with a pleasant laugh, the speaker entered the room. She was a girl of sixteen or thereabout, very beautiful, with very black hair and eyes. A face and form more entirely out of place you could not have found in the whole city. She sat herself at his feet, and, with her interlocked hands upon his knee, and her face, full of childish innocence mingled with womanly wisdom, turned to his, appeared for a time to take principal part in a conversation which, of course, could not be overheard in the corridor outside.

Whatever was said, she presently rose, he opened his arms, and she sat on his knee and kissed him. This done, there was a silence, both smiling pensively and gazing out over the rotten balcony into the street. After a while she started up, saying something about the change of weather, and, slipping away, thrust a match between the bars of the grate. The old man turned about to the fire, and she from her little room brought a low sewing-chair and sat beside him, laying her head on his knee, and he stroking her brow with his brown palm.

And then, in an altered—a low, sad tone—he be-gan a monotonous recital.

Thus they sat, he talking very steadily and she lis-tening, until all the neighborhood was wrapped in slumber,—all the neighbors, but not Kookoo.

Kookoo in his old age had become a great eaves-dropper; his ear and eye took turns at the keyhole that night, for he tells things that were not intended for outside hearers. He heard the girl sobbing, and the old man saying, "But you must go now. You cannot stay with me safely or decently, much as I wish it. The Lord only knows how I'm to bear it, or where you're to go; but He's your Lord, child, and He'll make a place for you. I was your grandfather's death; I frittered your poor, dead mother's fortune away : let that be the last damage I do.

"I have always meant everything for the best," he added half in soliloquy.

From all Kookoo could gather, he must have been telling her the very story just recounted. She had dropped quite to the floor, hiding her face in her hands, and was saying between her sobs, "I can-not go, Papa George ; oh, Papa George, I cannot go!"

Just then 'Sieur George, having kept a good reso-lution all day, was encouraged by the orphan's pitiful tones to contemplate the most senseless act he ever at-tempted to commit. He said to the sobbing girl that she was not of his blood ; that she was nothing to him by natural ties ; that his covenant was with her grand-sire to care for his offspring ; and though it had been poorly kept, it might be breaking it worse than ever to turn her out upon ever so kind a world.

"I have tried to be good to you all these years. When I took you, a wee little baby, I took you for better or worse. I intended to do well by you all your childhood-days, and to do best at last. I thought surely we should be living well by this time, and you could choose from a world full of homes and a world full of friends.

"I don't see how I missed it!" Here he paused a moment in meditation, and presently resumed with some suddenness:

"I thought that education, far better than Mother Nativity has given you, should have afforded your sweet charms a noble setting; that good mothers and sisters would be wanting to count you into their fami-∴es, and that the blossom of a happy womanhood would open perfect and full of sweetness.

"I would have given my life for it. I did give it, such as it was; but it was a very poor concern, I know — my life — and not enough to buy any good thing.

"I have had a thought of something, but I'm afraid to tell it. It didn't come to me to-day or yesterday; it has beset me a long time — for months."

The girl gazed into the embers, listening intensely.

"And oh! dearie, if I could only get you to think the same way, you might stay with me then."

"How long?" she asked, without stirring.

"Oh, as long as heaven should let us. But there is only one chance," he said, as it were feeling his way,

" only one way for us to stay together. Do you understand me? "

She looked up at the old man with a glance of painful inquiry.

" If you could be — my wife, dearie? "

She uttered a low, distressful cry, and, gliding swiftly into her room, for the first time in her young life turned the key between them.

And the old man sat and wept.

Then Kookoo, peering through the keyhole, saw that they had been looking into the little trunk. The lid was up, but the back was toward the door, and he could see no more than if it had been closed.

He stooped and stared into the aperture until his dry old knees were ready to crack. It seemed as if 'Sieur George was stone, only stone couldn't weep like that.

Every separate bone in his neck was hot with pain. He would have given ten dollars — ten sweet dollars! — to have seen 'Sieur George get up and turn that trunk around.

There! 'Sieur George rose up — what a face!

He started toward the bed, and as he came to the trunk he paused, looked at it, muttered something about " ruin," and something about " fortune," kicked the lid down and threw himself across the bed.

Small profit to old Kookoo that he went to his own couch; sleep was not for the little landlord. For well-nigh half a century he had suspected his tenant of having a treasure hidden in his house, and to-night he had heard his own admission that in the little trunk

was a fortune. Kookoo had never felt so poor in all
his days before. He felt a Creole's anger, too, that a
tenant should be the holder of wealth while his landlord suffered poverty.

And he knew very well, too, did Kookoo, what the
tenant would do. If he did not know what he kept in
the trunk, he knew what he kept behind it, and he
knew he would take enough of it to-night to make him
sleep soundly.

No one would ever have supposed Kookoo capable
of a crime. He was too fearfully impressed with the
extra-hazardous risks of dishonesty; he was old, too,
and weak, and, besides all, intensely a coward. Nevertheless, while it was yet two or three hours before
daybreak, the sleep-forsaken little man arose, shuf-
fled into his garments, and in his stocking-feet sought
the corridor leading to 'Sieur George's apartment.
The November night, as it often does in that region,
had grown warm and clear; the stars were sparkling
like diamonds pendent in the deep blue heavens, and
at every window and lattice and cranny the broad,
bright moon poured down its glittering beams upon
the hoary-headed thief, as he crept along the moulder-
ing galleries and down the ancient corridor that led to
'Sieur George's chamber.

'Sieur George's door, though ever so slowly opened,
protested with a loud creak. The landlord, wet with
cold sweat from head to foot, and shaking till the
floor trembled, paused for several minutes, and then
entered the moon-lit apartment. The tenant, lying as
if he had not moved. was sleeping heavily And now

the poor coward trembled so, that to kneel before the trunk, without falling, he did not know how. Twice, thrice, he was near tumbling headlong. He became as cold as ice. But the sleeper stirred, and the thought of losing his opportunity strung his nerves up in an instant. He went softly down upon his knees, laid his hands upon the lid, lifted it, and let in the intense moonlight. The trunk was full, full, crowded down and running over full, of the tickets of the Havana Lottery!

A little after daybreak, Kookoo from his window saw the orphan, pausing on the corner. She stood for a moment, and then dove into the dense fog which had floated in from the river, and disappeared. He never saw her again.

But her Lord is taking care of her. Once only she has seen 'Sieur George. She had been in the belvedere of the house which she now calls home, looking down upon the outspread city. Far away southward and westward the great river glistened in the sunset. Along its sweeping bends the chimneys of a smoking commerce, the magazines of surplus wealth, the gardens of the opulent, the steeples of a hundred sanctuaries and thousands on thousands of mansions and hovels covered the fertile birthright arpents which 'Sieur George, in his fifty yea s' stay, had seen tricked away from dull colonial Esaus by their blue-eyed brethren of the North. Nearer by she looked upon the forlornly silent region of lowly dwellings, neglected ny legislation and shunned by all lovers of comfort, that once had been the smiling fields of her own grand-

sire's broad plantation; and but a little way off, trudg-
ing across the marshy commons, her eye caught sight
of 'Sieur George following the sunset out upon the
prairies to find a night's rest in the high grass.

She turned at once, gathered the skirt of her pink
calico uniform, and, watching her steps through her
tears, descended the steep winding-stair to her frequent kneeling-place under the fragrant candles of the
chapel-altar in Mother Nativity's asylum.

'Sieur George is houseless. He cannot find the orphan. Mother Nativity seems to know nothing of
her. If he could find her now, and could get from her
the use of ten dollars for but three days, he knows a
combination which would repair all the past; it could
not fail, he — thinks. But he cannot find her, and
the letters he writes — all containing the one scheme
— disappear in the mail-box, and there's an end.

Madame Délicieuse

MADAME DELICIEUSE

Just adjoining the old Café de Poésie on the corner, stood the little one-story, yellow-washed tenement of Dr. Mossy, with its two glass doors protected by batten shutters, and its low, weed-grown tile roof sloping out over the sidewalk. You were very likely to find the Doctor in, for he was a great student and rather negligent of his business — as business. He was a small, sedate, Creole gentleman of thirty or more, with a young-old face and manner that provoked instant admiration. He would receive you — be you who you may — in a mild, candid manner, looking into your face with his deep blue eyes, and re-assuring you with a modest, amiable smile, very sweet and rare on a man's mouth.

To be frank, the Doctor's little establishment was dusty and disorderly — very. It was curious to see the jars, and jars, and jars. In them were serpents and hideous fishes and precious specimens of many sorts. There were stuffed birds on broken perches; and dried lizards, and eels, and little alligators, and old skulls with their crowns sawed off, and ten thousand odd scraps of writing-paper strewn with crumbs

of lonely lunches, and interspersed with long-lost spat-
ulas and rust-eaten lancets.

All New Orleans, at least all Creole New Orleans,
knew, and yet did not know, the dear little Doctor.
So gentle, so kind, so skilful, so patient, so lenient;
so careless of the rich and so attentive to the poor; a
man, all in all, such as, should you once love him, you
would love him forever. So very learned, too, but
with apparently no idea of how to *show himself* to his
social profit, — two features much more smiled at than
respected, not to say admired, by a people remote
from the seats of learning, and spending most of their
esteem upon animal heroisms and exterior display.

"Alas!" said his wealthy acquaintances, "what a
pity; when he might as well be rich."

"Yes, his father has plenty."

"Certainly, and gives it freely. But intends his
son shall see none of it."

"His son? You dare not so much as mention
him."

"Well, well, how strange! But they can never
agree — not even upon their name. Is not that droll?
— a man named General Villivicencio, and his son,
Dr. Mossy!"

"Oh, that is nothing; it is only that the Doctor
drops the *de Villivicencio.*"

"Drops the *de Villivicencio?* but I think the *de
Villivicencio* drops him, ho, ho, ho, — *diable!*"

Next to the residence of good Dr. Mossy towered
the narrow, red-brick-front mansion of young Madame
Délicieuse, firm friend at once and always of those two

antipodes, General Villivicencio and Dr. Mossy Its
dark, covered carriage-way was ever rumbling, and,
with nightfall, its drawing-rooms always sent forth a
luxurious light from the lace-curtained windows of the
second-story balconies.

It was one of the sights of the Rue Royale to see
by night its tall, narrow outline reaching high up to
ward the stars, with all its windows aglow.

The Madame had had some tastes of human experience; had been betrothed at sixteen (to a man she
did not love, "being at that time a fool," as she
said) ; one summer day at noon had been a bride, and
at sundown — a widow. Accidental discharge of the
tipsy bridegroom's own pistol. Pass it by ! It left
but one lasting effect on her, a special detestation of
quarrels and weapons.

The little maidens whom poor parentage has doomed
to sit upon street door-sills and nurse their infant
brothers have a game of "choosing" the beautiful
ladies who sweep by along the pavement; but in Rue
Royale there was no choosing; every little damsel
must own Madame Délicieuse or nobody, and as that
richly adorned and regal favorite of old General Villivicencio came along they would lift their big, bold
eyes away up to her face and pour forth their admiration in a universal — "Ah-h-h-h ! "

But, mark you, she was good Madame Délicieuse as
well as fair Madame Délicieuse : her principles, however, not constructed in the austere Anglo-Saxon style,
exactly (what. need, with the lattice of the Confessional not a stone's -throw off?). Her kind offices and

beneficent schemes were almost as famous as General
Villivicencio's splendid alms ; if she could at times do
what the infantile Washington said he could not, why
no doubt she and her friends generally looked upon it
as a mere question of enterprise.

She had charms, too, of intellect—albeit not such
a sinner against time and place as to be an "educated
woman"—charms that, even in a plainer person,
would have brought down the half of New Orleans
upon one knee, with both hands on the left side. *She*
had the *whole* city at her feet, and, with the fine tact
which was the perfection of her character, kept it there
contented. Madame was, in short, one of the kind that
gracefully wrest from society the prerogative of doing
as they please, and had gone even to such extravagant
lengths as driving out in the *Américain* faubourg,
learning the English tongue, talking national politics,
and similar freaks whereby she provoked the unbounded worship of her less audacious lady friends.
In the centre of the cluster of Creole beauties which
everywhere gathered about her, and, most of all, in
those incomparable companies which assembled in her
own splendid drawing-rooms, she was always queen
lily. *Her* house, *her* drawing-rooms, etc. ; for the
little brown aunt who lived with her was a mere piece
of curious furniture.

There was this notable charm about Madame Délicieuse, she improved by comparison. She never looked
so grand as when, hanging on General Villivicencio's
arm at some gorgeous ball, these two bore down on
you like a royal barge lashed to a ship-of-the-line

She never looked so like her sweet name, as when she seated her prettiest lady adorers close around her, and got them all a-laughing.

Of the two balconies which overhung the *banquette* on the front of the Délicieuse house, one was a small affair, and the other a deeper and broader one, from which Madame and her ladies were wont upon gala days to wave handkerchiefs and cast flowers to the friends in the processions. There they gathered one Eighth of January morning to see the military display. It was a bright blue day, and the group that quite filled the balcony had laid wrappings aside, as all flower-buds are apt to do on such Creole January days, and shone resplendent in spring attire.

The sight-seers passing below looked up by hundreds and smiled at the ladies' eager twitter, as, flirting in humming-bird fashion from one subject to another, they laughed away the half-hours waiting for the pageant. By and by they fell a-listening, for Madame Délicieuse had begun a narrative concerning Dr. Mossy. She sat somewhat above her listeners, her elbow on the arm of her chair, and her plump white hand waving now and then in graceful gesture, they silently attending with eyes full of laughter and lips starting apart.

" *Vous savez,*" she said (they conversed in French of course), " you know it is now long that Dr. Mossy and his father have been in disaccord. Indeed, when have they not differed? For, when Mossy was but a little boy, his father thought it hard that he was not ι rowdy. He switched him once because he would not

play with his toy gun and drum. He was not so high
when his father wished to send him to Paris to enter
the French army; but he would not go. We used to
play often together on the *banquette* — for I am not
so very many years younger than he, no indeed — and,
if I wanted some fun, I had only to pull his hair and
run into the house; he would cry, and monsieur papa
would come out with his hand spread open and " —

Madame gave her hand a malicious little sweep, and
joined heartily in the laugh which followed.

"That was when they lived over the way. But
wait! you shall see: I have something. This evening
the General " —

The houses of Rue Royale gave a start and rattled
their windows. In the long, irregular line of balconies
the beauty of the city rose up. Then the houses
jumped again and the windows rattled; Madame steps
inside the window and gives a message which the
housemaid smiles at in receiving. As she turns the
houses shake again, and now again; and now there
comes a distant strain of trumpets, and by and by
the drums and bayonets and clattering hoofs, and
plumes and dancing banners; far down the long street
stretch out the shining ranks of gallant men, and the
fluttering, over-leaning swarms of ladies shower down
their sweet favors and wave their countless welcomes.

In the front, towering above his captains, rides General Villivicencio, veteran of 1814–15, and, with the
gracious pomp of the old-time gentleman, lifts his
cocked hat, and bows, and bows.

Madame Délicieuse's balcony was a perfect maze of

waving kerchiefs. The General looked up for the woman of all women; she was not there. But he remembered the other balcony, the smaller one, and cast his glance onward to it. There he saw Madame and one other person only. A small blue-eyed, broad-browed, scholarly-looking man whom the arch lady had lured from his pen by means of a mock professional summons, and who now stood beside her, a smile of pleasure playing on his lips and about his eyes.

" *Vite!* " said Madame, as the father's eyes met the son's. Dr. Mossy lifted his arm and cast a bouquet of roses. A girl in the crowd bounded forward, caught it in the air, and, blushing, handed it to the plumed giant. He bowed low, first to the girl, then to the balcony above; and then, with a responsive smile, tossed up two splendid kisses, one to Madame, and one, it seemed —

" For what was that cheer? "

" Why, did you not see? General Villivicencio cast a kiss to his son. "

The staff of General Villivicencio were a faithful few who had not bowed the knee to any abomination of the Américains, nor sworn deceitfully to any species of compromise; their beloved city was presently to pass into the throes of an election, and this band, heroically unconscious of their feebleness, putting their trust in "re-actions" and like delusions, resolved to make one more stand for the traditions of their fathers. It was concerning this that Madame Délicieuse was incidentally about to speak when interrupted by the boom of

cannon; they had promised to meet at her house that
evening.

They met. With very little discussion or delay (for
their minds were made up beforehand), it was decided
to announce in the French-English newspaper that, at
a meeting of leading citizens, it had been thought
consonant with the public interest to place before the
people the name of General Hercule Mossy de Villivicencio. No explanation was considered necessary.
All had been done in strict accordance with time-hon-
ored customs, and if any one did not know it it was
his own fault. No eulogium was to follow, no editorial indorsement. The two announcements were des
tined to stand next morning, one on the English side
and one on the French, in severe simplicity, to be
greeted with profound gratification by a few old gentlemen in blue cottonade, and by roars of laughter
from a rampant majority.

As the junto were departing, sparkling Madame
Délicieuse detained the General at the head of the
stairs that descended into the tiled carriage-way, to
wish she was a man, that she might vote for him.

"But, General," she said, "had I not a beautiful
bouquet of ladies on my balcony this morning?"

The General replied, with majestic gallantry, that
"it was as magnificent as could be expected with the
central rose wanting." And so Madame was disappointed, for she was trying to force the General to
mention his son. "I will bear this no longer; he
shall not rest," she had said to her little aunt, "until
he has either kissed his son or quarrelled with him."

To which the aunt had answered that, "*coûte que coûte*, she need not cry about it;" nor did she. Though the General's compliment had foiled her thrust, she answered gayly to the effect that enough was enough; "but, ah! General," dropping her voice to an undertone, "if you had heard what some of those rosebuds said of you!"

The old General pricked up like a country beau. Madame laughed to herself, "Monsieur Peacock, I have thee;" but aloud she said gravely:

"Come into the drawing-room, if you please, and seat yourself. You must be greatly fatigued."

The friends who waited below overheard the invitation.

"*Au revoir, Général,*" said they.

"*Au revoir, Messieurs,*" he answered, and followed the lady.

"General," said she, as if her heart were overflowing, "you have been spoken against. Please sit down."

"Is that true, Madame?"

"Yes, General."

She sank into a luxurious chair.

"A lady said to-day — but you will be angry with me, General."

"With you, Madame? That is not possible."

"I do not love to make revelations, General; but when a noble friend is evil spoken of " — she leaned her brow upon her thumb and forefinger, and looked pensively at her slipper's toe peeping out at the edge of her skirt on the rich carpet — "one's heart gets very big."

"Madame, you are an angel! But what said she, Madame?"

"Well, General, I have to tell you the whole truth, if you will not be angry. We were all speaking at once of handsome men. She said to me: 'Well, Madame Délicieuse, you may say what you will of General Villivicencio, and I suppose it is true; but everybody knows'— pardon me, General, but just so she said—'all the world knows he treats his son very badly.'"

"It is not true," said the General.

"If I wasn't angry!" said Madame, making a pretty fist. 'How can that be?' I said. 'Well,' she said, 'mamma says he has been angry with his son for fifteen years.' 'But what did his son do?' I said. 'Nothing,' said she. '*Ma foi*,' I said, 'me, I too would be angry if my son had done nothing for fifteen years' — ho, ho, ho!"

"It is not true," said the General.

The old General cleared his throat, and smiled as by compulsion.

"You know, General," said Madame, looking distressed, "it was nothing to joke about, but I had to say so, because I did not know what your son had done, nor did I wish to hear any thing against one who has the honor to call you his father."

She paused a moment to let the flattery take effect, and then proceeded:

"But then another lady said to me; she said, 'For shame, Clarisse, to laugh at good Dr. Mossy; nobody - neither General Villivicencio, neither any other, has a right to be angry against that noble, gentle, kind, brave ' "—

"Brave!" said the General, with a touch of irony.

"So she said," answered Madame Délicieuse, "and I asked her, 'how brave?' 'Brave?' she said, 'why, braver than *any soldier*, in tending the small-pox, the cholera, the fevers, and all those horrible things. Me, I saw his father once run from a snake; I think *he* wouldn't fight the small-pox—my faith!' she said, 'they say that Dr. Mossy does all that and never wears a scapula!—and does it nine hundred and ninety-nine times in a thousand for nothing! *Is* that brave, Madame Délicieuse, or is it not?'—And, General,—what could I say?"

Madame dropped her palms on either side of her spreading robes and waited pleadingly for an answer. There was no sound but the drumming of the General's fingers on his sword-hilt. Madame resumed:

"I said, 'I do not deny that Mossy is a noble gentleman;'—I had to say that, had I not, General?"

"Certainly, Madame," said the General, "my son is a gentleman, yes."

"'But,' I said, 'he should not make Monsieur, his father, angry.'"

"True," said the General, eagerly.

"But that lady said: 'Monsieur, his father, makes himself angry,' she said. 'Do you know, Madame, why his father is angry so long?' Another lady says, 'I know!' 'For what?' said I. 'Because he refused to become a soldier; mamma told me that.' 'It cannot be!' I said."

The General flushed. Madame saw it, but relent-
lessly continued:

"'*Mais oui*,' said that lady. 'What!' I said,
'think you General Villivicencio will not rather be the
very man most certain to respect a son who has the
courage to be his own master? Oh, what does he
want with a poor fool of a son who will do only as he
says? You think he will love him less for healing
instead of killing? Mesdemoiselles, you do not know
that noble soldier!'"

The noble soldier glowed, and bowed his acknowledgments in a dubious, half remonstrative way, as if
Madame might be producing material for her next
confession, as, indeed, she diligently was doing; but
she went straight on once more, as a surgeon would.

"But that other lady said: 'No, Madame, no, ladies:
but I am going to tell you why Monsieur, the General,
is angry with his son.' 'Very well, why?'—'Why?
It is just—because—he is—a little man!'"

General Villivicencio stood straight up.

"Ah! mon ami," cried the lady, rising excitedly,
"I have wounded you and made you angry, with my
silly revelations. Pardon me, my friend. Those were
foolish girls, and, anyhow, they admired you. They
said you looked glorious—grand—at the head of the
procession."

Now, all at once, the General felt the tremendous
fatigues of the day; there was a wild, swimming,
whirling sensation in his head that forced him to let
his eyelids sink down; yet, just there, in the midst
of his painful bewilderment, he realized with ecstatic

complacency that the most martial-looking man in Louisiana was standing in his spurs with the hand of Louisiana's queenliest woman laid tenderly on his arm.

"I am a wretched tattler!" said she.

"Ah! no, Madame, you are my dearest friend, yes.'

"Well, anyhow, I called them fools. 'Ah! innocent creatures,' I said, 'think you a man of his sense and goodness, giving his thousands to the sick and afflicted, will cease to love his only son because he is not big like a horse or quarrelsome like a dog? No, ladies, there is a great reason which none of you know.' 'Well, well,' they cried, 'tell it; he has need of a very good reason; tell it now.' 'My ladies,' I said, 'I must not' — for, General, for all the world I knew not a reason why you should be angry against your son; you know, General, you have never told me."

The beauty again laid her hand on his arm and gazed, with round-eyed simplicity, into his sombre countenance. For an instant her witchery had almost conquered.

"Nay, Madame, some day I shall tell you; I have more than one burden *here*. But let me ask you to be seated, for I have a question, also, for you, which I have longed to ask. It lies heavily upon my heart; I must ask it now. A matter of so great importance " —

Madame's little brown aunt gave a faint cough from a dim corner of the room.

" 'Tis a beautiful night," she remarked, and stepped out on the balcony.

Then the General asked his question. It was a very long question, or, maybe, repeated twice or thrice ; for it was fully ten minutes before he moved out of the room, saying good-evening.

Ah! old General Villivicencio. The most martial-looking man in Louisiana! But what would the people, the people who cheered in the morning, have said, to see the fair Queen Délicieuse at the top of the stair, sweetly bowing you down into the starlight, — humbled, crestfallen, rejected!

The campaign opened. The Villivicencio ticket was read in French and English with the very different sentiments already noted. In the Exchange, about the courts, among the "banks," there was lively talking concerning its intrinsic excellence and extrinsic chances. The young gentlemen who stood about the doors of the so-called "coffee-houses" talked with a frantic energy alarming to any stranger, and just when you would have expected to see them jump and bite large mouthfuls out of each other's face, they would turn and enter the door, talking on in the same furious manner, and, walking up to the bar, click their glasses to the success of the Villivicencio ticket. Sundry swarthy and wrinkled remnants of an earlier generation were still more enthusiastic. There was to be a happy renaissance ; a purging out of Yankee ideas ; a blessed home-coming of those good old Bourbon morals and manners which Yankee notions had expatriated. In the cheerfulness of their anticipations they even went the length of throwing their feet high in air, thus indicating how the Villivi-cencio ticket was going to give "doze Américains" the kick under the nose.

In the three or four weeks which followed, the General gathered a surfeit of adulation, notwithstand-ing which he was constantly and with pain imagining a confused chatter of ladies, and when he shut his eyes with annoyance, there was Madame Délicieuse standing, and saying, "I knew not a reason why you should be angry against your son," gazing in his face with hardened simplicity, and then — that last scene on the stairs wherein he seemed still to be descending, down, down.

Madame herself was keeping good her resolution.

"Now or never," she said, "a reconciliation or a quarrel."

When the General, to keep up appearances, called again, she so moved him with an account of certain kindly speeches of her own invention, which she im-puted to Dr. Mossy, that he promised to call and see his son; "perhaps;" "pretty soon;" "probably."

Dr. Mossy, sitting one February morning among his specimens and books of reference, finishing a thrilling chapter on the cuticle, too absorbed to hear a door open, suddenly realized that something was in his light, and, looking up, beheld General Villivicencio standing over him. Breathing a pleased sigh, he put down his pen, and, rising on tiptoe, laid his hand upon his father's shoulder, and lifting his lips like a little wife, kissed him.

"Be seated, papa," he said, offering his own chair, and perching on the desk.

The General took it, and, clearing his throat, gazed around upon the jars and jars with their little Adams and Eves in zoölogical gardens.

" Is all going well, papa? " finally asked Dr. Mossy.

" Yes."

Then there was a long pause.

" 'Tis a beautiful day," said the son.

" Very beautiful," rejoined the father.

" I thought there would have been a rain, but it has cleared off," said the son.

" Yes," responded the father, and drummed on the desk.

" Does it appear to be turning cool? " asked the son.

" No; it does not appear to be turning cool at all," was the answer.

" H'm 'm ! " said Dr. Mossy.

" Hem ! " said General Villivicencio.

Dr. Mossy, not realizing his own action, stole a glance at his manuscript.

" I am interrupting you,' said the General, quickly, and rose.

" No, no ! pardon me ; be seated ; it gives me great pleasure to — I did not know what I was doing.   It is the work with which I fill my leisure moments."

So the General settled down again, and father and son sat very close to each other — in a bodily sense ; spiritually they were many miles apart. The General's finger-ends, softly tapping the desk, had the sound of far-away drums.

" The city — it is healthy? " asked the General.

"Did you ask me if"—said the little Doctor, starting and looking up.

"The city—it has not much sickness at present?" repeated the father.

"No, yes—not much," said Mossy, and, with utter unconsciousness, leaned down upon his elbow and supplied an omitted word to the manuscript.

The General was on his feet as if by the touch of a spring.

"I must go!"

"Ah! no, papa," said the son.

"But, yes, I must."

"But wait, papa, I had just now something to speak of"—

"Well?" said the General, standing with his hand on the door, and with rather a dark countenance.

Dr. Mossy touched his fingers to his forehead, trying to remember.

"I fear I have—ah! I rejoice to see your name before the public, dear papa, and at the head of the ticket."

The General's displeasure sank down like an eagle's feathers. He smiled thankfully, and bowed.

"My friends compelled me," he said.

"They think you will be elected?"

"They will not doubt it. But what think you, my son?"

Now the son had a conviction which it would have been madness to express, so he only said:

"They could not elect one more faithful."

The General bowed solemnly.

"Perhaps the people will think so; my friends believe they will."

"Your friends who have used your name should help you as much as they can, papa," said the Doctor. "Myself, I should like to assist you, papa, if I could."

"A-bah!" said the pleased father, incredulously.

"But, yes," said the son.

A thrill of delight filled the General's frame. *This was* like a son.

"Thank you, my son! I thank you much. Ah, Mossy, my dear boy, you make me happy!"

"But," added Mossy, realizing with a tremor how far he had gone, "I see not how it is possible."

The General's chin dropped.

"Not being a public man," continued the Doctor; "unless, indeed, my pen — you might enlist my pen."

He paused with a smile of bashful inquiry. The General stood aghast for a moment, and then caught the idea.

"Certainly! cer-tain-ly! ha, ha, ha!" — backing out of the door — "certainly! Ah! Mossy, you are right, to be sure; to make a complete world we must have swords *and* pens. Well, my son, ' *au revoir;* ' no, I cannot stay — I will return. I hasten to tell my friends that the pen of Dr. Mossy is on our side! Adieu, dear son."

Standing outside on the *banquette* he bowed — not to Dr. Mossy, but to the balcony of the big red-brick front — a most sunshiny smile, and departed.

The very next morning, as if fate had ordered it, the Villivicencio ticket was attacked — ambushed, as it were, from behind the Américain newspaper. The onslaught was—at least General Villivicencio said it was—absolutely ruffianly. Never had all the lofty courtesies and formalities of chivalric contest been so completely ignored. Poisoned balls—at least personal epithets—were used. The General himself was called " antiquated ! " The friends who had nominated him, they were positively sneered at ; dubbed "fossils," " old ladies," and their caucus termed "irresponsible "—thunder and lightning ! gentlemen of honor to be termed "not responsible ! " It was asserted that the nomination was made secretly, in a private house, by two or three unauthorized harum-scarums (that touched the very bone) who had with more caution than propriety withheld their names. The article was headed, " The Crayfish-eaters' Ticket." It continued further to say that, had not the publication of this ticket been regarded as a dull hoax, it would not have been suffered to pass for two weeks unchallenged, and that it was now high time the universal wish should be realized in its withdrawal.

Among the earliest readers of this production was the young Madame. She first enjoyed a quiet gleeful smile over it, and then called :

" Ninide, here, take this down to Dr. Mossy—stop." She marked the communication heavily with her gold pencil. " No answer ; he need not return it."

About the same hour, and in a neighboring street, one of the "not responsibles" knocked on the Villi-vicencio castle gate. The General invited him into his bedroom. With a short and strictly profane harangue the visitor produced the offensive newspaper, and was about to begin reading, when one of those loud nasal blasts, so peculiar to the Gaul, resounded at the gate, and another "not responsible" entered, more excited, if possible, than the first. Several minutes were spent in exchanging fierce sentiments and slapping the palm of the left hand rapidly with the back of the right. Presently there was a pause for breath.

"Alphonse, proceed to read," said the General, sitting up in bed.

"De Crayfish-eaters' Ticket"—began Alphonse; but a third rapping at the gate interrupted him, and a third "irresponsible" re-enforced their number, talking loudly and wildly to the waiting-man as he came up the hall.

Finally, Alphonse read the article. Little by little the incensed gentlemen gave it a hearing, now two words and now three, interrupting it to rip out long, rasping maledictions, and wag their forefingers at each other as they strode ferociously about the apartment.

As Alphonse reached the close, and dashed the paper to the floor, the whole quartet, in terrific unison, cried for the blood of the editor.

But hereupon the General spoke with authority.

"No, Messieurs," he said, buttoning his dressing-gown, savagely, "you shall not fight him. I forbid it —you shall not!"

"But," cried the three at once, "one of us must fight, and you— you cannot; if *you* fight our cause is lost! The candidate must not fight."

"Hah-h! Messieurs," cried the hero, beating his breast and lifting his eyes, "*grace au ciel.* I have a son. Yes, my beloved friends, a son who shall call the villain out and make him pay for his impudence with blood, or eat his words in to-morrow morning's paper. Heaven be thanked that gave me a son for this occasion! I shall see him at once — as soon as I can dress."

"We will go with you."

"No, gentlemen, let me see my son alone. I can meet you at Maspero's in two hours. Adieu, my dear friends."

He was resolved.

"*Au revoir,*" said the dear friends.

Shortly after, cane in hand, General Villivicencio moved with an ireful stride up the *banquette* of Rue Royale. Just as he passed the red-brick front one of the batten shutters opened the faintest bit, and a certain pair of lovely eyes looked after him, without any of that round simplicity which we have before discovered in them. As he half turned to knock at his son's door he glanced at this very shutter, but it was as tightly closed as though the house were an enchanted palace.

Dr. Mossy's door, on the contrary, swung ajar when he knocked, and the General entered.

"Well, my son, have you seen that newspaper? No, I think not. I *see* you have not, since your cheeks are not red with shame and anger."

Dr. Mossy looked up with astonishment from the desk where he sat writing.

"What is that, papa?"

"My faith! Mossy, is it possible you have not heard of the attack upon me, which has surprised and exasperated the city this morning?"

"No," said Dr. Mossy, with still greater surprise, and laying his hand on the arm of his chair.

His father put on a dying look. "My soul!" At that moment his glance fell upon the paper which had been sent in by Madame Délicieuse. "But, Mossy, my son," he screamed, "*there* it is!" striking it rapidly with one finger — "there! there! there! read it! It calls me 'not responsible!' 'not responsible' it calls me! Read! read!"

"But, papa," said the quiet little Doctor, rising, and accepting the crumpled paper thrust at him, "I have read this. If this is it, well, then, already I am preparing to respond to it."

The General seized him violently, and, spreading a suffocating kiss on his face, sealed it with an affectionate oath.

"Ah, Mossy, my boy, you are glorious! You had begun already to write! You are glorious! Read to me what you have written, my son."

The Doctor took up a bit of manuscript, and resuming his chair, began:

"Messrs. Editors: On your journal of this morning" —

"Eh! how! you nave not written it in English, is it, son?"

"But, yes, papa."

"'Tis a vile tongue," said the General; "but, if it is necessary — proceed."

"Messrs. Editors: On your journal of this morning is published an editorial article upon the Villivicencio ticket, which is plentiful and abundant with mistakes. Who is the author or writer of the above said editorial article your corre spondent does at present ignore, but doubts not he is one who, hasty to form an opinion, will yet, however, make his assent to the correction of some errors and mistakes which " —

"Bah!" cried the General.

Dr. Mossy looked up, blushing crimson.

"Bah!" cried the General, still more forcibly. "Bêtise!"

"How?" asked the gentle son.

"'Tis all nonsent!" cried the General, bursting into English. "Hall you 'ave to say is: ''Sieur Editeurs! I want you s'all give de nem of de in-dignan' scoundrel who meck some lies on you' paper about mon père et ses amis!"

"Ah-h!" said Dr. Mossy, in a tone of derision and anger.

His father gazed at him in mute astonishment. He stood beside his disorderly little desk, his small form drawn up, a hand thrust into his breast, and that look of invincibility in his eyes such as blue eyes sometimes surprise us with.

"You want me to fight," he said.

"My faith!" gasped the General, loosening in all his joints. "I believe — you may cut me in pieces if I do not believe you were going to reason it out in the newspaper! Fight? If I want you to fight? Upon my soul, I believe you do not want to fight!"

"No," said Mossy.

"My God!" whispered the General. His heart seemed to break.

"Yes," said the steadily gazing Doctor, his lips trembling as he opened them. "Yes, your God. I am afraid"—

"Afraid!" gasped the General.

"Yes," rang out the Doctor, "afraid; afraid! God forbid that I should not be afraid. But I will tell you what I do not fear—I do not fear to call your affairs of honor—murder!"

"My son!" cried the father.

"I retract," cried the son; "consider it unsaid. I will never reproach my father."

"It is well," said the father. "I was wrong. It is my quarrel. I go to settle it myself."

Dr. Mossy moved quickly between his father and the door. General Villivicencio stood before him utterly bowed down.

"What will you?" sadly demanded the old man.

"Papa," said the son, with much tenderness, "I cannot permit you. Fifteen years we were strangers, and yesterday were friends. You must not leave me so. I will even settle this quarrel for you. You must let me. I am pledged to your service."

The peace-loving little doctor did not mean "to settle," but "to adjust." He felt in an instant that he was misunderstood; yet, as quiet people are apt to do, though not wishing to deceive, he let the misinterpretation stand. In his embarrassment he did not know with absolute certainty what te should do himself.

The father's face—he thought of but one way to
settle a quarrel—began instantly to brighten. "I
would myself do it," he said, apologetically, "but my
friends forbid it."

"And so do I," said the Doctor, "but I will go
myself now, and will not return until all is finished
Give me the paper."

"My son, I do not wish to compel you."

There was something acid in the Doctor's smile as
he answered:

"No; but give me the paper, if you please."

The General handed it.

"Papa," said the son, "you must wait here for my
return."

"But I have an appointment at Maspero's at"—

"I will call and make excuse for you," said the
son.

"Well," consented the almost happy father, "go,
my son; I will stay. But if some of your sick shall
call?"

"Sit quiet," said the son. "They will think no
one is here." And the General noticed that the dust
lay so thick on the panes that a person outside would
have to put his face close to the glass to see within.

In the course of half an hour the Doctor had reached
the newspaper office, thrice addressed himself to the
wrong person, finally found the courteous editor, and
easily convinced him that his father had been imposed
upon; but when Dr. Mossy went farther, and asked
which one of the talented editorial staff had written
the article:

"You see, Doctor," said the editor — "just step into my private office a moment."

They went in together. The next minute saw Dr. Mossy departing hurriedly from the place, while the editor complacently resumed his pen, assured that he would not return.

General Villivicencio sat and waited among the serpents and innocents. His spirits began to droop again. Revolving Mossy's words, he could not escape the fear that possibly, after all, his son might compromise the Villivicencio honor in the interests of peace. Not that he preferred to put his son's life in jeopardy; he would not object to an adjustment, provided the enemy should beg for it. But if not, whom would his son select to perform those friendly offices indispensable in polite quarrels? Some half-priest, half-woman? Some spectacled book-worm? He suffered.

The monotony of his passive task was relieved by one or two callers who had the sagacity (or bad manners) to peer through the dirty glass, and then open the door, to whom, half rising from his chair, he answered, with a polite smile, that the Doctor was out, nor could he say how long he might be absent. Still the time dragged painfully, and he began at length to wonder why Mossy did not return.

There came a rap at the glass door different from all the raps that had forerun it — a fearless, but gentle, dignified, graceful rap; and the General, before he looked round, felt in all his veins that it came from the young Madame. Yes, there was her glorious outline thrown sidewise upon the glass. He hastened and threw open the door, bending low at the same instant, and extending his hand.

She extended hers also, but not to take his. With a calm dexterity that took the General's breath, she reached between him and the door, and closed it.

"What is the matter?" anxiously asked the General —for her face, in spite of its smile, was severe.

"General," she began, ignoring his inquiry—and, with all her Creole bows, smiles, and insinuating phrases, the severity of her countenance but partially waned—"I came to see my physician—your son. Ah! General, when I find you reconciled to your son, it makes me think I am in heaven. You will let me say so? You will not be offended with the old play-mate of your son?"

She gave him no time to answer.

"He is out, I think, is he not? But I am glad of it. It gives us occasion to rejoice together over his many merits. For you know, General, in all the years of your estrangement, Mossy had no friend like myself. I am proud to tell you so now; is it not so?"

The General was so taken aback that, when he had thanked her in a mechanical way, he could say nothing else. She seemed to fall for a little while into a sad meditation that embarrassed him beyond measure. But as he opened his mouth to speak, she resumed:

"Nobody knew him so well as I; though I, poor me, I could not altogether understand him; for look you, General, he was—what do you think?—*a great man!*—nothing less."

"How?" asked the General, not knowing what else to respond.

"You never dreamed of that, eh?" continued the lady "But, of course not; nobody did but me. Some of those Américains, I suppose, knew it; but who would ever ask them? Here in Royal Street, in New Orleans, where we people know nothing and care nothing but for meat, drink, and pleasure, he was only Dr. Mossy, who gave pills. My faith! General, no wonder you were disappointed in your son, for you thought the same. Ah! yes, you did! But why did you not ask me, his old playmate? I knew better. I could have told you how your little son stood head and shoulders above the crowd. I could have told you some things too wonderful to believe. I could have told you that his name was known and honored in the scientific schools of Paris, of London, of Germany! Yes! I could have shown you" — she warmed as she proceeded — "I could have shown you letters (I begged them of him), written as between brother and brother, from the foremost men of science and discovery!"

She stood up, her eyes flashing with excitement.

"But why did you never tell me?" cried the General.

"He never would allow me — but you — why did you not ask me? I will tell you; you were too proud to mention your son. But he had pride to match yours — ha! — achieving all — every thing — with an assumed name! 'Let me tell your father,' I implored him; but — 'let him find me out,' he said, and you never found him out. Ah! there he was fine He would not, he said, though only for your sake, re-enter your

affections as any thing more or less than just — your
son. Ha!"

And so she went on. Twenty times the old Gen
eral was astonished anew, twenty times was angry or
alarmed enough to cry out, but twenty times she would
not be interrupted. Once he attempted to laugh, but
again her hand commanded silence.

"Behold, Monsieur, all these dusty specimens, these
revolting fragments. How have you blushed to know
that our idle people laugh in their sleeves at these
things! How have you blushed — and you his father!
But why did you not ask me? I could have told you:
'Sir, your son is not an apothecary; not one of these
ugly things but has helped him on in the glorious path
of discovery; discovery, General — your son — known
in Europe as a scientific discoverer!' Ah-h! the blind
people say, 'How is that, that General Villivicencio
should be dissatisfied with his son? He is a good man,
and a good doctor, only a little careless, that's all.'
But *you* were more blind still, for you shut your eyes
tight like this; when, had you searched for his virtues
as you did for his faults, you, too, might have known
before it was too late what nobility, what beauty,
what strength, were in the character of your poor,
poor son!"

"Just Heaven! Madame, you shall not speak of
my son as of one dead and buried! But, if you have
some bad news" —

"Your son took your quarrel on his hands, eh?"

"I believe so — I think" —

"Well; I saw him an hour ago in search of our
erer!"

"He must find him!" said the General, plucking up.

"But if the search is already over," slowly responded Madame.

The father looked one instant in her face, then rose with an exclamation:

"Where is my son? What has happened? Do you think I am a child, to be trifled with — a horse to be teased? Tell me of my son!"

Madame was stricken with genuine anguish.

"Take your chair," she begged; "wait; listen; take your chair."

"Never!" cried the General; "I am going to find my son — my God! Madame, you have *locked this door!* What are you, that you should treat me so? Give me, this instant" —

"Oh! Monsieur, I beseech you to take your chair, and I will tell you all. You can do nothing now. Listen! suppose you should rush out and find that your son had played the coward at last! Sit down and" —

"Ah! Madame, this is play!" cried the distracted man.

"But no; it is not play. Sit down; I want to ask you something."

He sank down and she stood over him, anguish and triumph strangely mingled in her beautiful face.

"General, tell me true; did you not force this quarrel into your son's hand? I *know* he would not choose to have it. Did you not do it to test his courage, because all these fifteen years you have made yourself a fool with the fear that he became a student only to escape being a soldier? Did you not?"

Her eyes looked him through and through.

"And if I did?" demanded he with faint defiance.

"Yes! and if he has made dreadful haste and proved his courage?" asked she.

"Well, then," — the General straightened up triumphantly — "then he is my son!"

He beat the desk.

"And heir to your wealth, for example?"

"Certainly."

The lady bowed in solemn mockery.

"It will make him a magnificent funeral!"

The father bounded up and stood speechless, trembling from head to foot. Madame looked straight in his eye.

"Your son has met the writer of that article."

"Where?" the old man's lips tried to ask.

"Suddenly, unexpectedly, in a passage-way."

"My God! and the villain" —

"Lives!" cried Madame.

He rushed to the door, forgetting that it was locked. "Give me that key!" he cried, wrenched at the knob, turned away bewildered, turned again toward it, and again away; and at every step and turn he cried, "Oh! my son, my son! I have killed my son! Oh! Mossy, my son, my little boy! Oh! my son, my son!'

Madame buried her face in her hands and sobbed aloud. Then the father hushed his cries and stood for a moment before her.

"Give me the key, Clarisse, let me go."

She rose and laid her face on his shoulder.

'What is it, Clarisse?'' asked he.

"Your son and I were ten years betrothed.''

"Oh, my child!''

"Because, being disinherited, he would not be my husband.''

"Alas! would to God I had known it! Oh! Mossy. my son.''

"Oh! Monsieur,'' cried the lady, clasping her hands, "forgive me — mourn no more — your son is unharmed! *I* wrote the article — I am your recanting slanderer! Your son is hunting for me now. I told my aunt to misdirect him. I slipped by him unseen in the carriage-way.''

The wild old General, having already staggered back and rushed forward again, would have seized her in his arms, had not the little Doctor himself at that instant violently rattled the door and shook his finger at them playfully as he peered through the glass.

"Behold!'' said Madame, attempting a smile: "open to your son; here is the key.''

She sank into a chair.

Father and son leaped into each other's arms; then turned to Madame:

"Ah! thou lovely mischief-maker'' —

She had fainted away.

"Ah! well, keep out of the way, if you please, papa,'' said Dr. Mossy, as Madame presently reopened her eyes; "no wonder you fainted; you have finished some hard work — see; here; so; Clarisse dear, take this.'

Father and son stood side by side, tenderly regarding her as she revived.

"Now, papa, you may kiss her; she is quite herself again, already."

"My daughter!" said the stately General; "this —is my son's ransom; and, with this,—I withdraw the Villivicencio ticket."

"You shall not," exclaimed the laughing lady, throwing her arms about his neck.

"But, yes!" he insisted; "my faith! you will at least allow me to remove my dead from the field."

"But, certainly;" said the son; "see, Clarisse, here is Madame, your aunt, asking us all into the house. Let us go."

The group passed out into the Rue Royale, Dr. Mossy shutting the door behind them. The sky was blue, the air was soft and balmy, and on the sweet south breeze, to which the old General bared his grateful brow, floated a ravishing odor of—

"Ah! what is it?" the veteran asked of the younger pair, seeing the little aunt glance at them with a playful smile.

Madame Délicieuse for almost the first time in her life, and Dr. Mossy for the thousandth—blushed.

It was the odor of orange-blossoms.

VOODOO IN NEW ORLEANS

By Robert Tallant

"Straightforward handling of . . . voodooism in all its manifestations." **Kirkus Reviews**

Originally published in 1946, this intriguing book examines the rites and beliefs associated with voodoo through the legends of the art—its charms, trances, rituals, and difficult-to-explain occurrences.

The lives of New Orleans' most infamous witch doctors and voodoo queens have been re-created in this well-researched account of New Orleans' dark underworld.

256 pp. 4¼ x 7 3rd pb ptg.
ISBN-13: 9780882893365 $5.95 pb

THE VOODOO QUEEN

By Robert Tallant

"Exceedingly well executed."　　　　**New York Times**

"It is an absorbing tale, and the emotional undertones, the conflicts in her human relations, the overwhelming loneliness of her position, all come through in the story of a strange life."　　　**Kirkus Reviews**

Accused of unspeakable crimes by some and regarded as almost saintly by others, Marie Laveau, Queen of the Voodoos, is considered to have been the most important voodooienne ever to ply her trade.

320 pp. 4¼ x 7 2nd ptg.
ISBN-13: 9780882893327 $7.99 pb

FABULOUS NEW ORLEANS

By Lyle Saxon

From Mardi Gras through the eyes of a child to the Great Flood of the Mississippi River in 1927, Lyle Saxon documents many of the quirks and mysteries of New Orleans. He gives a history of the city and detailed accounts of Louisiana's strange and remarkable happenings, including the year of the great plague and voodoo ceremonies. Saxon captures the image of a city steeped in the traditions and idiosyncrasies of French, Spanish, and American cultures, with all of the city's flaws and glories.

400 pp. 6 x 9 81 b/w illus. Index
ISBN-13: 9780882897066 $14.95 pb

NEW ORLEANS AS IT WAS

By Henry C. Castellanos

First published in 1895, New Orleans as It Was vividly records episodes of antebellum Louisiana life and includes pivotal eras in the city's history. Henry C. Castellanos describes the events at the Old Parish Prison and the successful transition into a new era by Mayor Louis Philippe Roffignac. This volume is a delightful tribute to New Orleans history not found in textbooks.

350 pp. 5½ x 8¼ 9 b/w illus. Index
ISBN-13: 9780882897875 $12.95 pb

OLD LOUISANA

By Lyle Saxon

Lyle Saxon, one of Louisiana's foremost authors, chronicles much of the state's history, from the early French settlers and the later Spanish rulers to the rise and collapse of the great plantation era. The reader meets daring pioneers, hot-tempered duelists, aristocratic planters, rough-hewn river men, and Creole beauties. Bringing to light old diaries, letters, and other rare sources, Saxon creates a sensitive and realistic portrait of this charming, colorful state and its people.

448 pp. 6 x 9 67 b/w illus. Index
ISBN-13: 9780882897059 $14.95 pb

THE DEVIL'S BACKBONE: The Story of the Natchez Trace

By Jonathan Daniels

The Natchez Trace has as dark and bloody a history as any thoroughfare since the beginning of our nation. Author Jonathan Daniels takes the reader over the old trail, exploring the whole dramatic story of the Natchez Trace in fascinating detail.

Here is a story of the men and women who crossed a wilderness to build America, moving ever onward for God, for glory, and for gold.

272 pp. $4^{1}/_{4}$ x 7 4th pb ptg.
ISBN-13: 9780882894386 $6.95 pb

SOUTHERN LIBRARY SERIES

HUEY LONG'S LOUISIANA HAYRIDE
  by Harnett T. Kane

GUMBO YA-YA: FOLK TALES OF LOUISIANA
  by Lyle Saxon, Edward Dreyer, and Robert Tallant

OLD LOUISIANA by Lyle Saxon

FABULOUS NEW ORLEANS by Lyle Saxon

LAFITTE THE PIRATE by Lyle Saxon

CHILDREN OF STRANGERS by Lyle Saxon

MARDI GRAS . . . AS IT WAS by Robert Tallant

THE PIRATE LAFITTE AND THE
  BATTLE OF NEW ORLEANS
  by Robert Tallant

EVANGELINE AND THE ACADIANS
  by Robert Tallant

NEW ORLEANS AS IT WAS
  by Henry C. Castellanos

OLD NEW ORLEANS:
  WALKING TOURS OF THE FRENCH QUARTER
  by Stanley Clisby Arthur

MARDI GRAS: A PICTORIAL HISTORY OF
  CARNIVAL IN NEW ORLEANS
  by Leonard V. Huber

END OF AN ERA: NEW ORLEANS, 1850-1860
  by Robert C. Reinders